Greatest Crafts & Projects for Children

Vikas khatri

Published by:

F-2/16, Ansari Road, Daryaganj, New Delhi-110002
☎ 011-23240026, 011-23240027 • *Fax:* 011-23240028
Email: info@vspublishers.com • *Website:* www.vspublishers.com

Branch: Hyderabad
5-1-707/1, Brij Bhawan (Beside Central Bank of India Lane)
Bank Street, Koti, Hyderabad - 500 095
☎ 040-24737290
E-mail: vspublishershyd@gmail.com

Follow us on:

All books available at **www.vspublishers.com**

© Copyright: V&S PUBLISHERS
ISBN 978-93-815883-2-1
Edition: 2012

The Copyright of this book, as well as all matter contained herein (including illustrations) rests with the Publisher. No person shall copy the name of the book, its title design, matter and illustrations in any form and in any language, totally or partially or in any form. Anybody doing so shall face legal action and will be responsible for damages.

Printed at : Pushp Print, Moujpur, New Delhi

Publisher's Note

All kids are creative and we are here to make them realise and cultivate the creativity within themselves.

The reasons to craft with your kids are virtually endless – discovery, wonder, exploration, creativity, learning, bonding, and simple gift of your time. And what better way to spend time with your kids than doing an activity that's not only fun but also promotes creativity and self-expression?

So, we present **Greatest Crafts and Projects for Children** to keep little hands busy day after day – inspiring and creative projects for kids of all ages and skill levels. Every project includes step-by-step instructions and lists of materials, skills, and time needed. The projects are unique but simple, so all parents, educators, caregivers and children can easily make them. Materials for each project are easy-to-find and inexpensive, most of which are available at home. Simple techniques learned from this book will encourage children to create many more projects of their own. Sometimes a little help or guidance from parents, teachers and mentors may be necessary, but help should be kept to a minimum to enable the child to get maximum satisfaction from the finished result.

Get creative with kids!!!

Contents

Publisher's Note   3
How to Enlarge Instruction Diagrams   7

1. Doggy Dog   8
2. Cloth Bag   10
3. Potato Prints and Leaf Prints   12
4. Octopus, Elephant and Seal   14
5. Spinning Spirals and Walk-Along Dragon   16
6. Bookmark and Felt Oven Gloves   18
7. Silver Bird   20
8. Silhouette Theatre   22
9. Making the Roof (Part 2)   24
10. Softy Soft Toy   26
11. "Snakey" the Draught Excluder and Desk Tidy   28
12. Three Dimensional Picture and Mosaic Picture   30
13. Clown Stick Puppet   32
14. Garden Landscape (Part 3)   34
15. Outdoor Noughts & Crosses and Whipping Top   36
16. Table Decoration   38
17. 'Lace' Picture Frame and Felt Pictures   40
18. Sock-Head Clown and Puppet Theatre   42
19. Garden Furniture and Pool (Part 4)   44
20. Potato Man with Hair that Grow and Rabbit with Ears that Grow   46
21. Montage Picture Calendar and Pop-Up Card   48
22. Collage Picture   50
23. Girl Dress-Up Doll   52
24. Lounge Furniture (Part 5)   54
25. Doll's Cradle   56
26. Paper Mats and Windmill   58
27. Pom Pom Cat and French Knitting   60
28. Rabbit and Witch Costumes   62
29. Bedroom Furniture (Part 6)   64
30. Spinner   66
31. Cotton Reel Caterpillar and Bottle Top Mobile (Wind Chime)   68
32. Pin Cushion and Paper Earrings   70
33. Fairy and Queen Costumes   72
34. Hall and Landing Furniture (Part 7)   74

35.	Cork Models	76
36.	Party Place Names and Party Sweet Tree	78
37.	Soft Toy and Melon-Seed Necklace	80
38.	Lion Costume	82
39.	Kitchen Furniture (Part 8)	84
40.	Doll's Shop and Nurse's Outfit	86
41.	Rose	88
42.	Book Cover and Construction Cards	90
43.	Bathroom Furniture (Part 9)	92
44.	Colour Spin and Carousel	94
45.	Sunflower and Dahlia	96
46.	Cotton Wool Snowman and Cotton Wool Chick	98
47.	Decorating the Rooms (Part 10)	100
48.	Magic Tree and Elephant Wall Frieze	102
49.	Lantern and Paper Necklace	104
50.	Apple Cat and Potato Hedgehog	106
51.	Egg Box Models	108
52.	Pressed Flower Pictures and Pressed Flower Greeting Card	110
53.	Kaleidoscope	112
54.	Jacob's Ladder	114

How to Enlarge Instruction Diagrams

Occasionally, in the instructions, you will find a diagram printed on a grid; this is to help you draw the required shape to the correct size. The following notes explain how to use the grid.

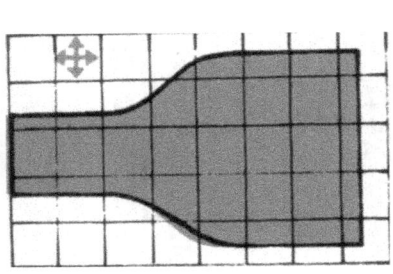 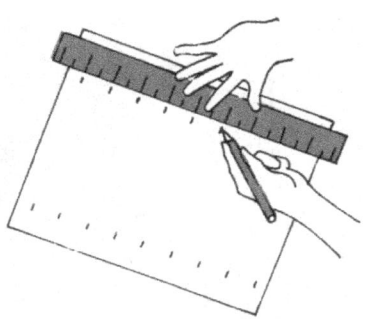 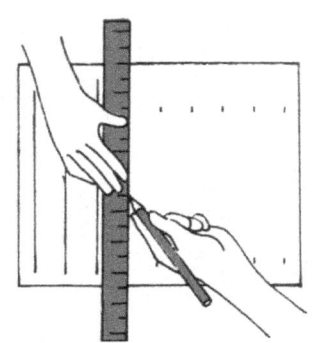

1. On the printed grid you will see the size of one square marked by arrows. This is the size each square must be when you draw your grid.
2. First mark out the correct number of upright lines near the top of your paper or card and then do the same near the bottom.
3. Pencil in the upright lines using a ruler to keep them straight.

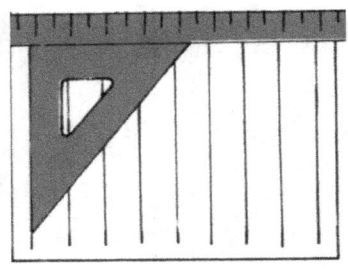 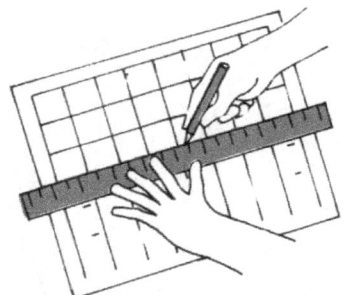 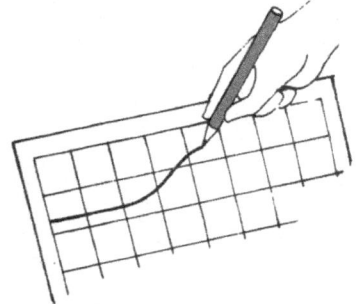

4. Use a set square to draw the top line of your grid. Place the ruler against it if it is not big enough.
5. Measure out the correct number of horizontal lines starting with the one you have just drawn, then pencil them in.
6. Now draw the shape onto your grid square by square. As an example, go back to drawing No. 1. You will see that the outline starts on the second square down. It goes horizontally across two squares, begins to go up on the third square, then goes right up into the top line at the fourth square and so on.

1
Doggy Dog

Materials Required

* Three Squares of stiff paper 6" × 6"
* Cotton Wool
* Glue

①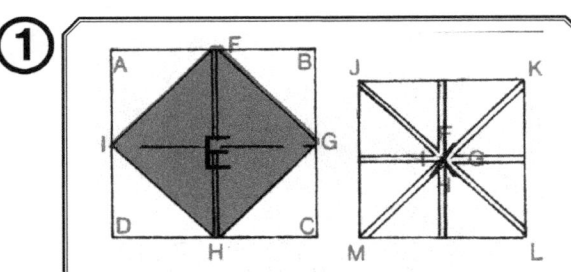
Fold points ABCD to point E. Turn over and fold points FGHI into centre as shown.

②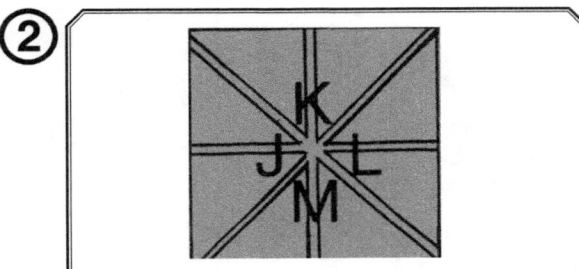
Turn over and fold points JKLM into centre as shown.

③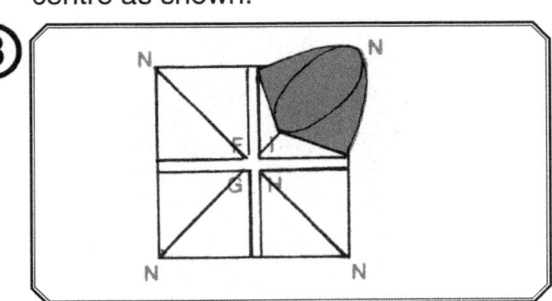
Turn over again and open out lines IN/HN/GN/FN as shown.

④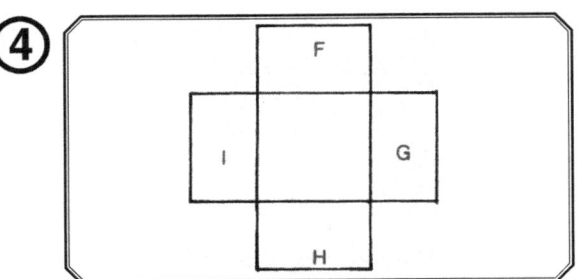
Now flatten out as diagram.

⑤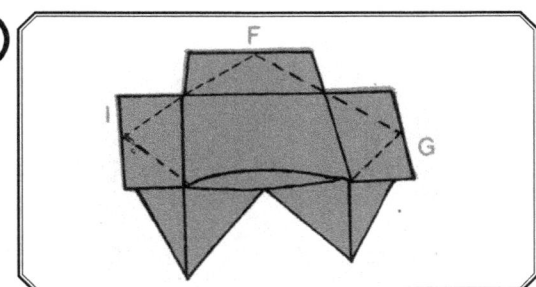
Fold points JKLM down as shown to make legs.

⑥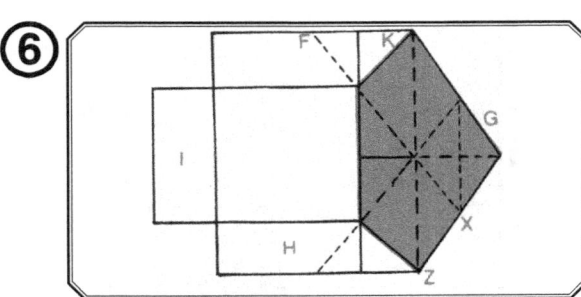
Now pull one side (G) out as shown and the opposite side (I).

⑦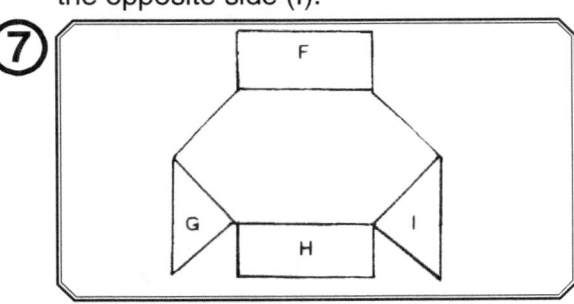
Fold along line FX and tuck in Z. Repeat on other side. Repeat instructions 1 to 7 for two more sections

⑧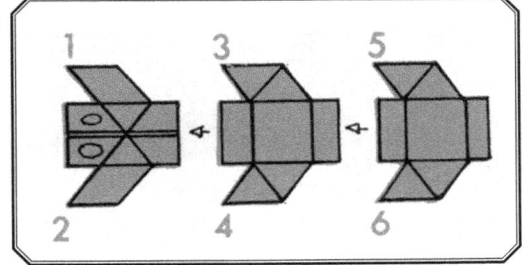
Fit the three sections together as shown, and decorate with cotton wool. Bend points 1,2 up for ears, 3, 4, 5 and 6 down for legs.

2

Cloth Bag

Materials Required

- Wire coat hanger
- Piece of strong cloth 32" × 16 "
- Two pieces of coloured ribbon 9" long
- Scissors, needle and thread

①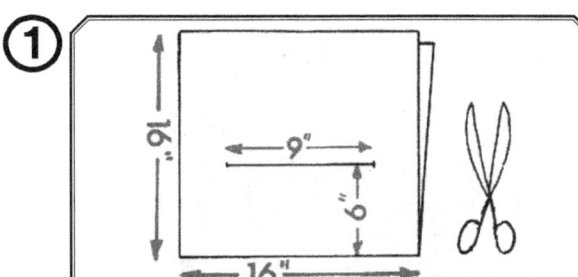
Fold the cloth in half. Cut a 9" slit as shown in one of the 16" squares.

②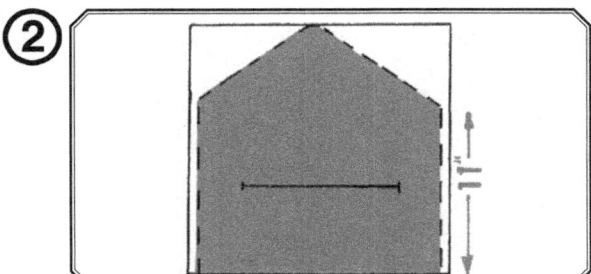
Sew both squares together, along dotted lines, with the best side inwards.

③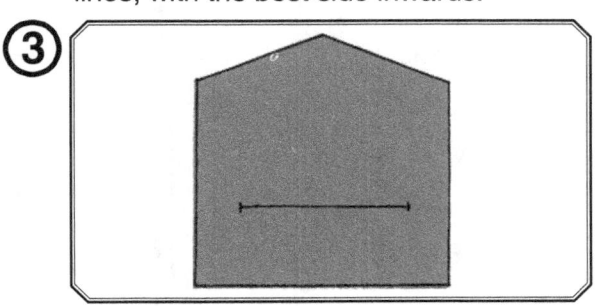
Cut off excess cloth, and turn bag inside out.

④
Make a small hole in the top for the hook of the cost hanger.

⑤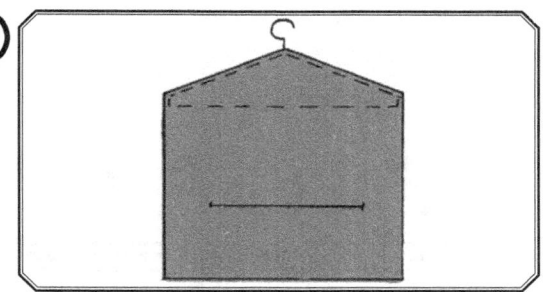
Put hanger inside bag through slit, and push hook through hole at top of bag.

⑥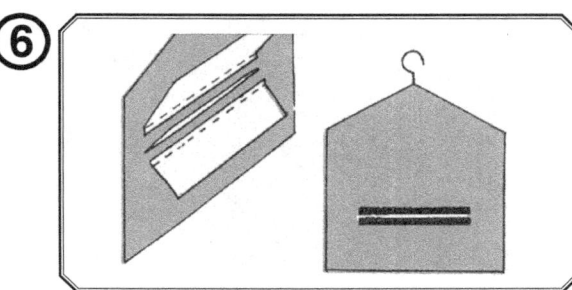
Sew the edges of the ribbons to the edges of the slits. Sew inside and outside.

⑦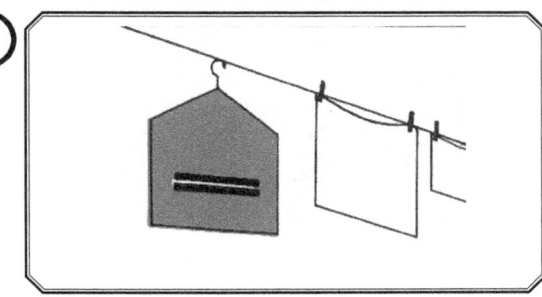
Your bag is now ready to fill with pegs and hang on the line.

⑧
You can also use your bag to keep your toys or shoes in.

3

Potato Prints and Leaf Prints

Materials Required

Potato Prints
* Potatoes – medium or large ones
* Paper
* Coloured paints
* Penknife

Leaf Prints
* Various Shaped leaves
* Large sheet of white paper
* Smaller piece of cardboard
* Coloured paints

Potato Prints

①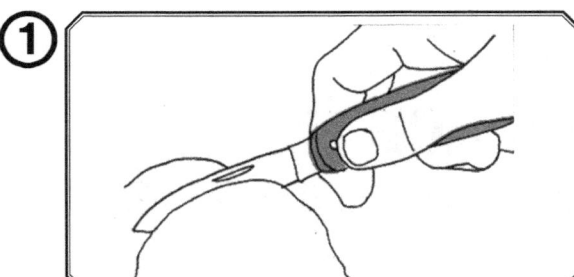
Cut a potato in half. Try to make sure that the cut is straight.

②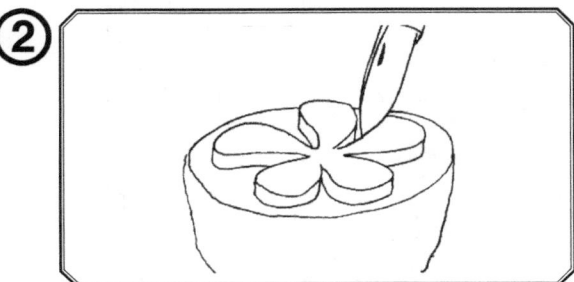
Carefully cut away part of the flat surface to leave a pattern or a letter.

③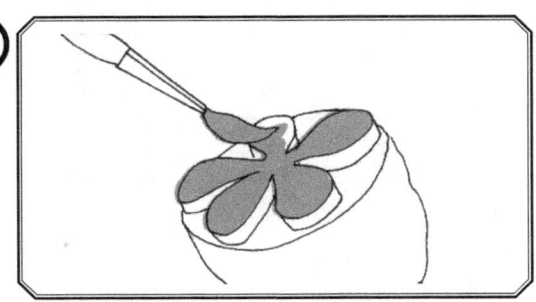
Brush paint onto the raised pattern in whatever colour you like (but not too much).

④
Press the potato on the paper. Use other designs and colours.

Leaf Prints

①
Collect as many different leaves as you can. If they are crinkly, flatten them in a book.

②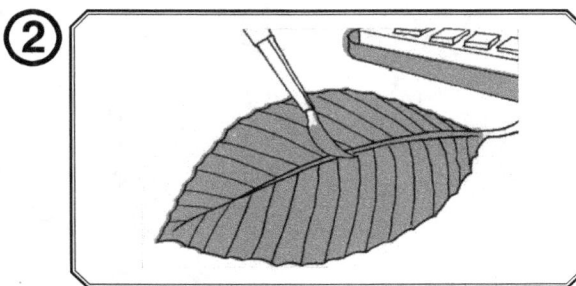
Take one leaf and paint it one colour. Don't put too much paint on!

③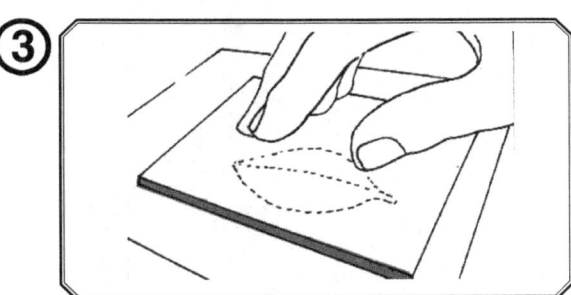
Let the paint get fairly dry. Use card to press the leaf, painted side down, on paper.

④
Paint more leaves in different colours. Press them on the paper until your picture is complete.

Octopus, Elephant and Seal

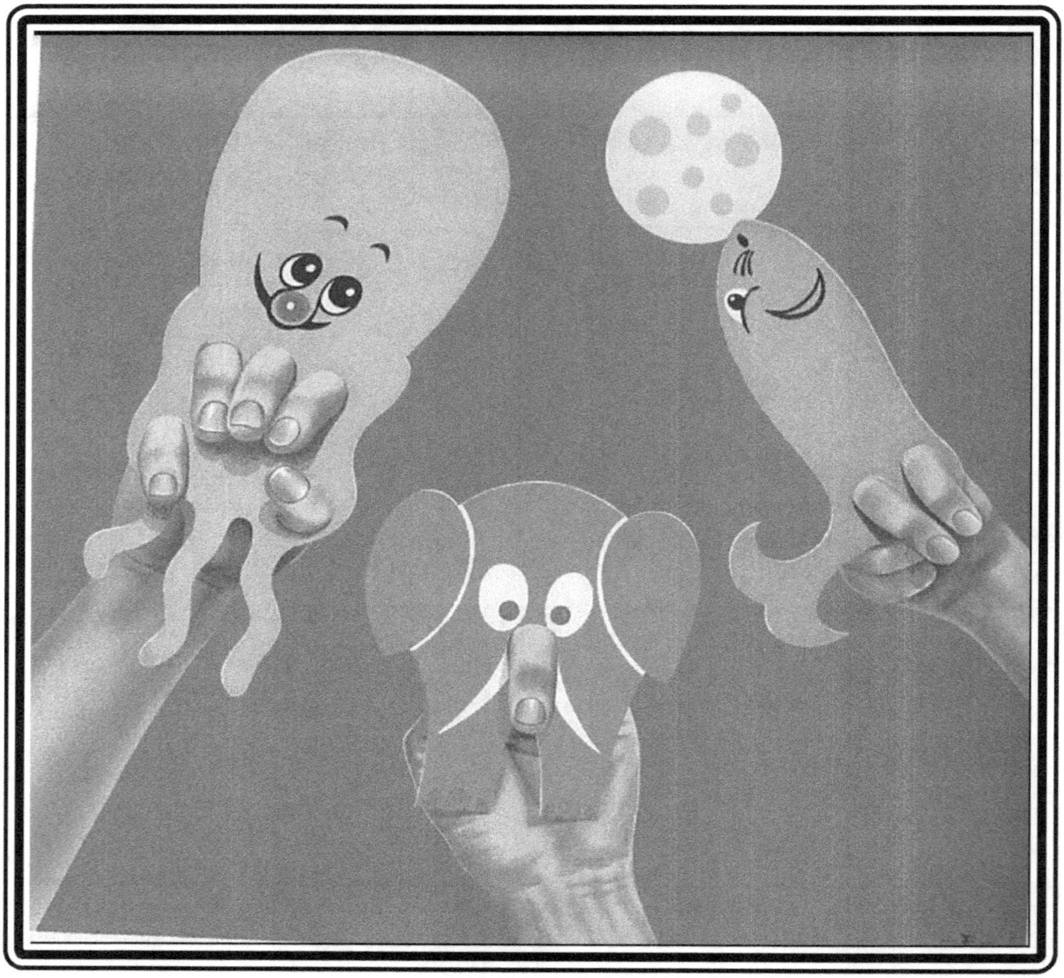

Materials Required

* Three pieces of thin cardboard or thick paper, about 4"× 6"
* Pencil
* Scissors
* Coloured paints

①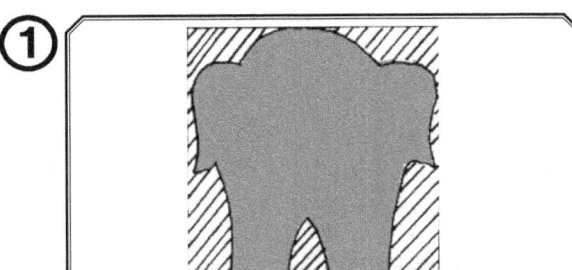
Draw pattern for the elephant on card or paper. Cut round the edges of the pattern.

②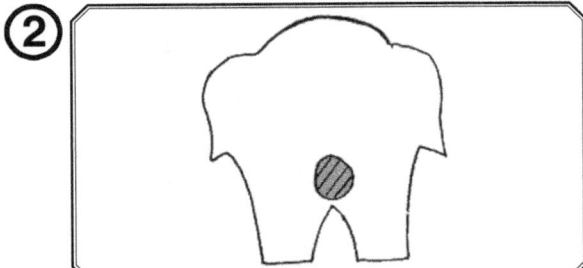
Cut a hole in the middle of the card large enough to put your finger through.

③
Paint on the eyes, tusks, and colour the rest of the body.

④
Put your finger through the hole from behind for the elephant's trunk.

⑤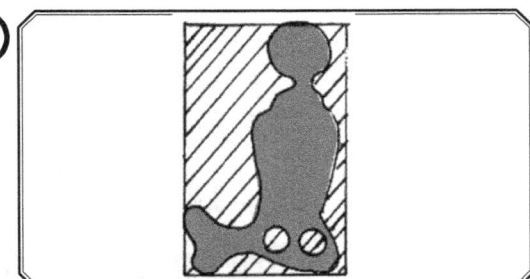
Draw and cut out the pattern for the seal. Make two holes at the bottom for flippers.

⑥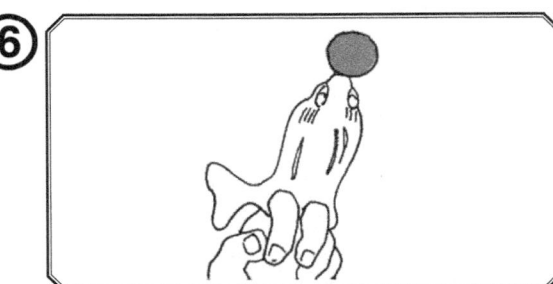
Decorate your seal with coloured paints, and let him perform.

⑦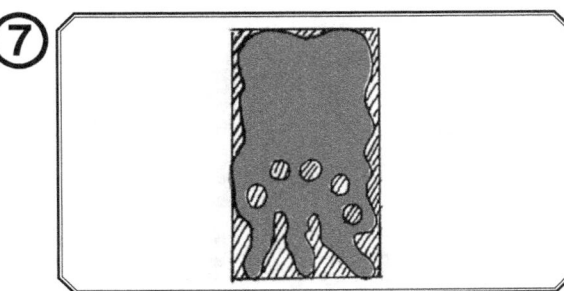
Draw and cut out pattern for the octopus. Make five holes at the bottom for his tentacles.

⑧
Decorate your octopus with coloured paints. Now he is ready to wriggle!

5
Spinning Spirals and Walk-Along Dragon

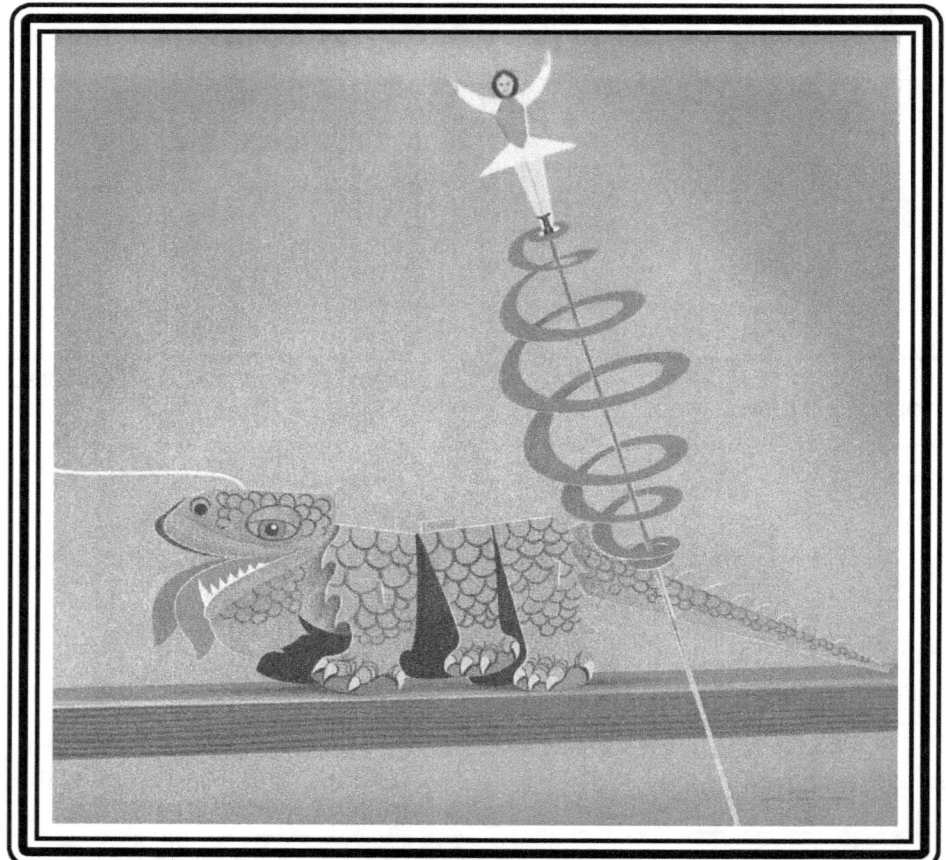

Materials Required

Spinning Spirals
* Two discs of paper 3" diameter
* Cork
* Knitting needle
* Piece of thin card 2"× 2"
* Pencil
* Scissors

Walk-Along Dragon
* Two piece of thin card 7½ × 9"
* Piece of string
* Pencil
* Scissors, good penknife
* Coloured paints
* Glue

Spinning Spirals

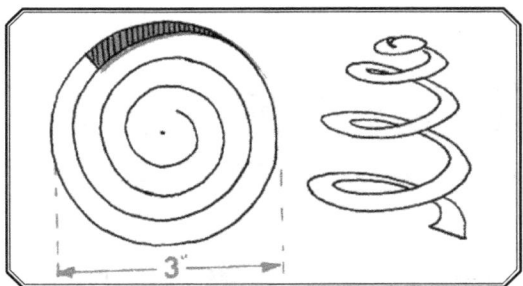

① Draw two spirals on the paper discs and cut them out.

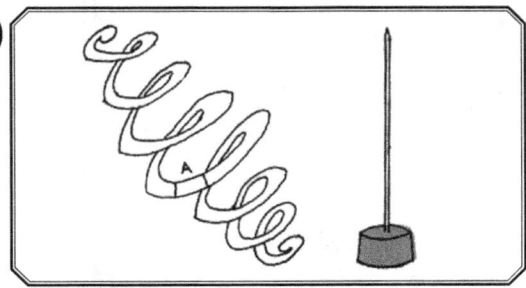

② Glue the spirals together at A. Stick knitting needle into cork.

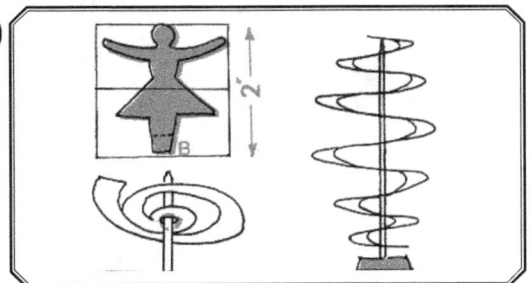

③ Draw and cut out dancer from 2" square of card. Make ¼" hole in centre of one spiral and put needle through.

④ Let needle just prick centre of other spiral. Glue dancer on top and watch her turn!

Walk-Along Dragon

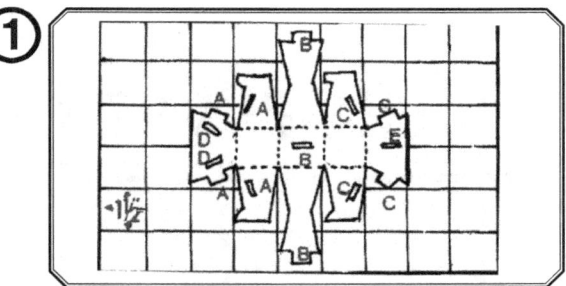

① Draw pattern on card. Cut it out and make slots where shown.

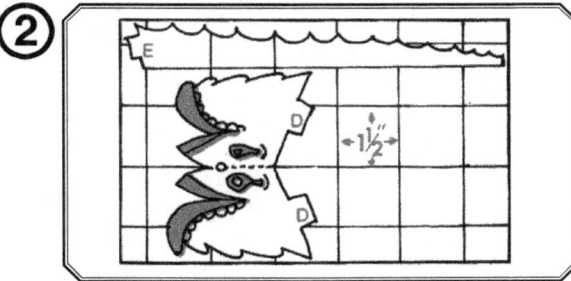

② Draw and cut patterns on other card for the dragon's head and tail.

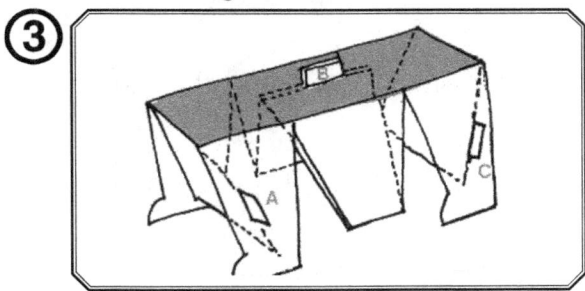

③ Insert tabs A into slots A, tabs B into slots B and tabs C into slots C.

④ Insert and glue tabs D into slots D and tab E into slot E. Attach string to head and pull gently.

6

Bookmark and Felt Oven Gloves

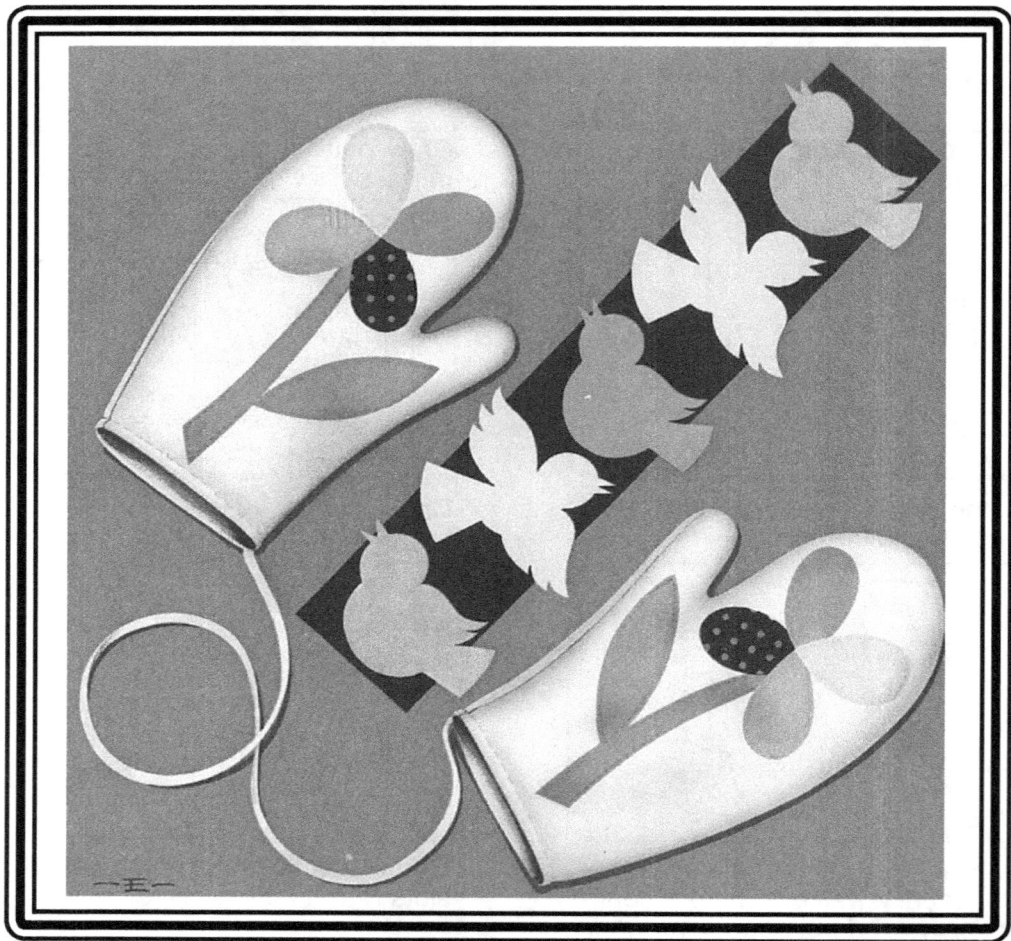

Materials Required

Bookmark
* Piece of coloured ribbon 8" long × 1 ½" wide or thin
* card
* Pieces of coloured paper or cloth
* Glue
* Pencil, scissors

Felt Oven Gloves
* Six pieces of thick felt,
* 9" long × 7½" wide
* Scraps of coloured cloth
* Cotton wool for stuffing
* Cloth tape 18" long × ½" wide
* Scissors, needle and thread

Bookmark

① Cut designs from coloured paper or cloth in the above shapes.

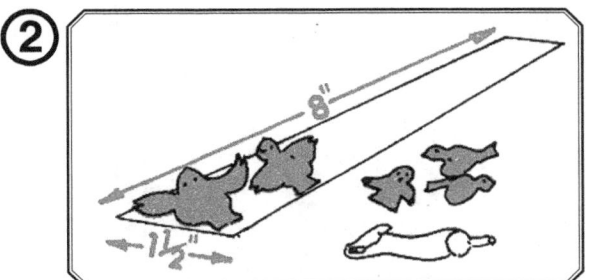

② Begin gluing them onto the ribbon or thin card.

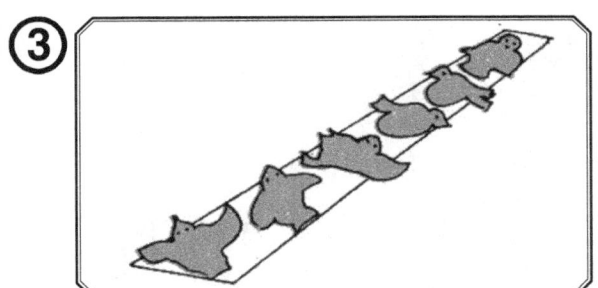

③ When you have a covered the ribbon or card your bookmark is complete.

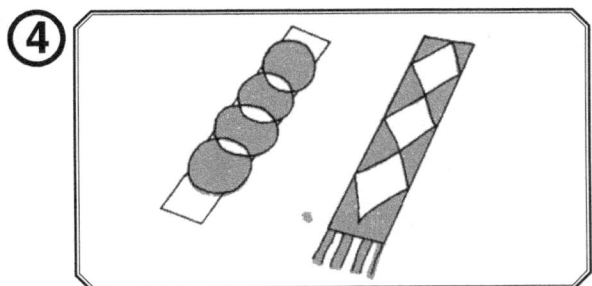

④ You can make more bookmarks using different shapes. Allow glue to dry before you put it in a book!

Felt Oven Gloves

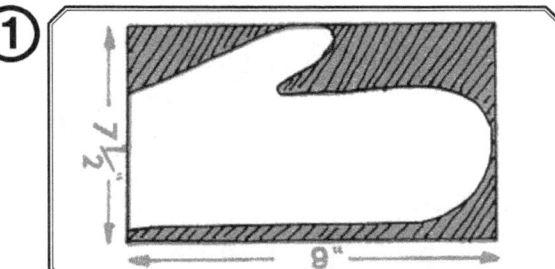

① Cut six felt patterns as shown. Stitch two pairs along the edges. Add one more to palm of each glove.

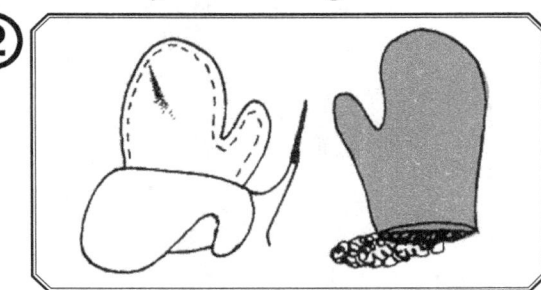

② Turn gloves inside out. Then stuff palms of gloves with cotton wool and sew together.

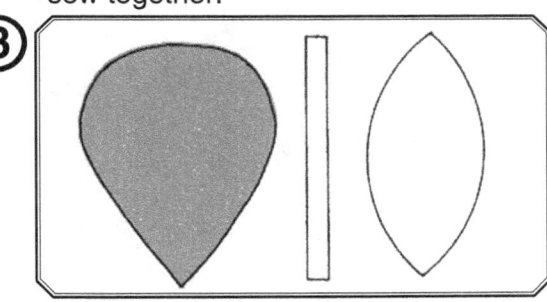

③ Cut petals and leaf shapes from scraps of coloured cloth. Sew them onto top of each glove.

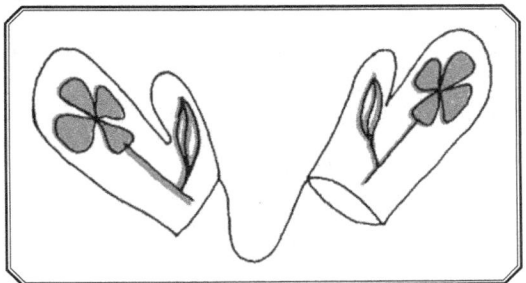

④ Sew ends of 18" cloth tape to each glove, just below the thumb.

7
Silver Bird

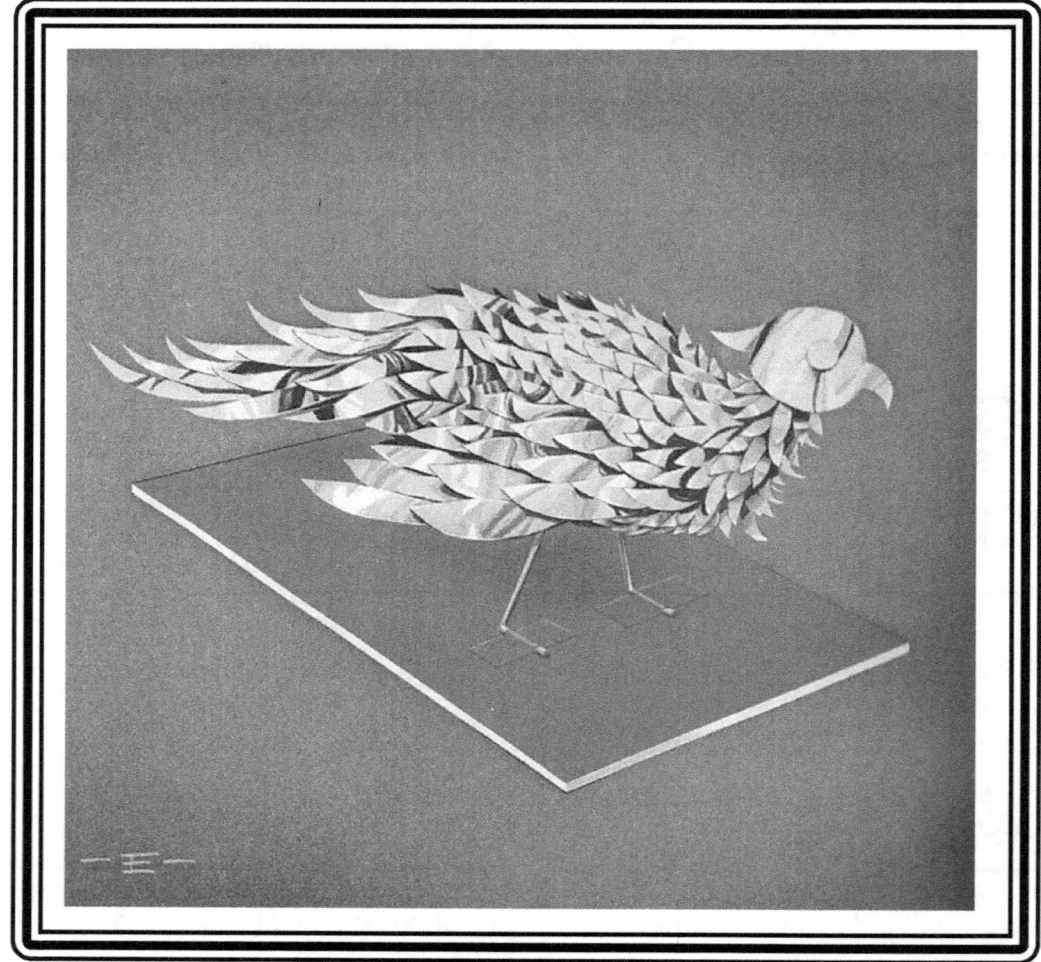

Materials Required

* Thin card 8" × 5"
* Newspapers
* Roll of tin foil
* Thick cardboard 17" × 7" for base
* Two pieces of thin card 5" × 2"
* Two large paper clips
* Cellotape
* Scissors
* Paint, glue

①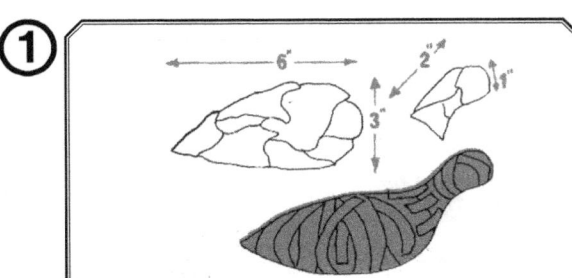
Crumble sheets of newspaper and bind them with tape to form the body and head of the bird.

②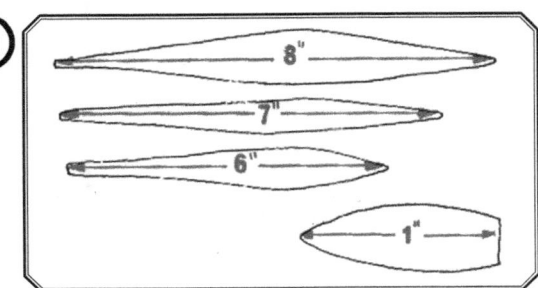
Cut patterns from card 8" X 5" for tail and body feather guides. Use these guides to cut the feathers from foil.

③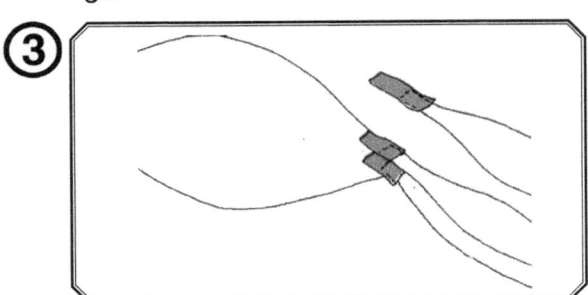
Tape two of each size tail feather to the end of the body, beginning with the longest.

④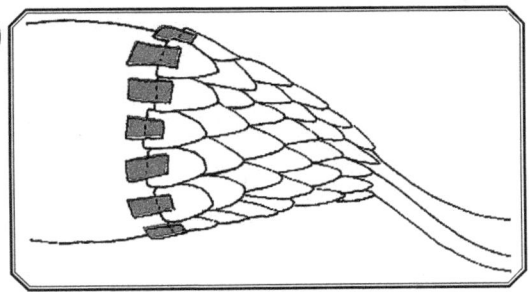
Cut dozens of body feathers. Tape them on as shown, beginning at the tail.

⑤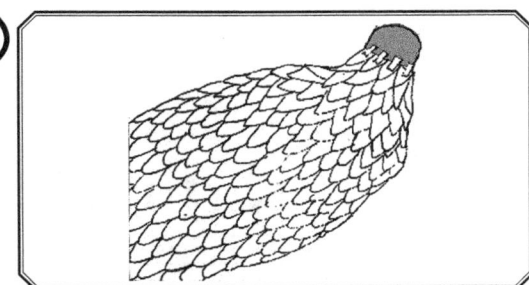
Continue until the whole body is covered. Leave area uncovered at top of neck.

⑥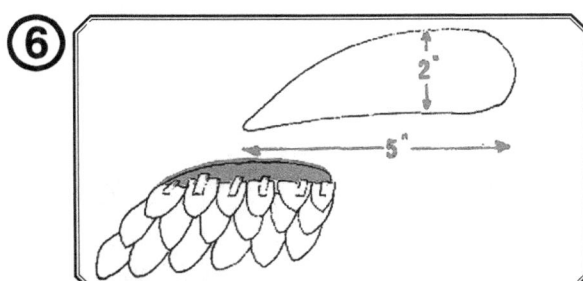
Draw and cut two patterns for wings from cards 5" X 2". Tape feathers to wing as shown, then tape wings to body.

⑦
Draw and cut pattern from foil for head. Fold along dotted line. Tape to neck. Glue on foil discs for eyes.

⑧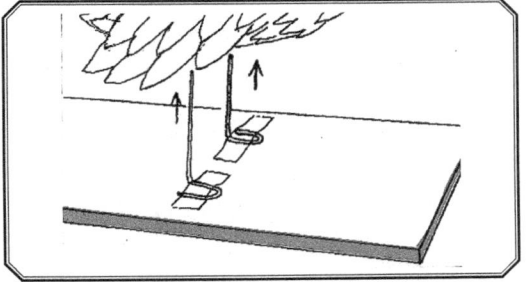
Straighten clips to make legs. Tape to baseboard in position. Push bird onto the two upright wires. Paint base.

8

Silhouette Theatre

Materials Required

* Piece of thick cardboard 33" × 20"
* Strip of cardboard 18" × 1½"
* Strip of cardboard 18" × 1"
* Two sheets of thin cardboard 8" × 5"
* Glue
* Scissors, Good penknife, coloured paints

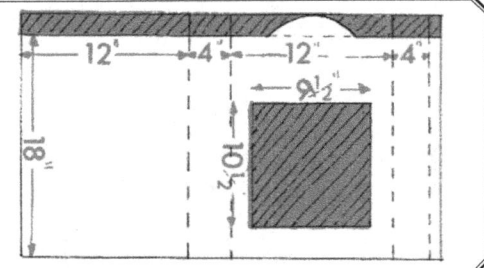 

1. Draw and cut out pattern for theatre from large piece of card. Fold along dotted lines.

5. Draw, cut out and paint the paper clown figure as shown.

  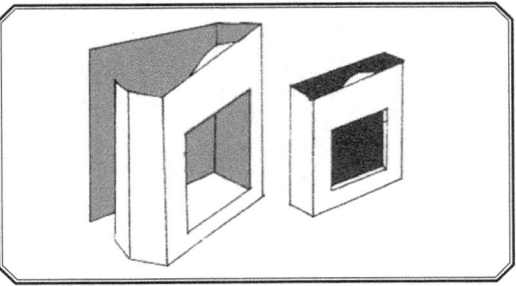 

2. Glue together as shown. Paint inside black, and paint bright colours on outside.

6. Draw, cut and paint the crazy cow.

  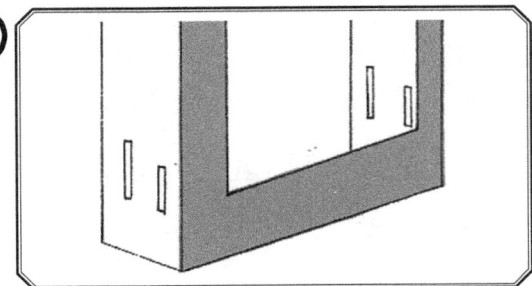 

3. Cut slots at each side, as shown. 1 ½" slot at back, 1" slot in front.

7. Glue the cow to the back strip of card, and the clown to the front.

  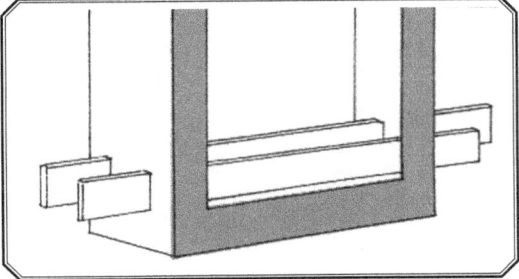 

4. Paint the 18" strips of card black, and push them through the slots.

8. Now move the figures from side to side across the stage. Make other characters and put on a show.

Making the Roof (Part 2)

Materials Required

* Two piece of thick cardboard or corrugated board 19" x 9 ½"
* Two pieces of thick cardboard or corrugated board 7 ¾ x 11 ½
* Two pieces of thin card 8½ x 4½
* Two pieces of thin card 1" x 1½"
* Tape, glue, scissors, penknife, coloured paints

①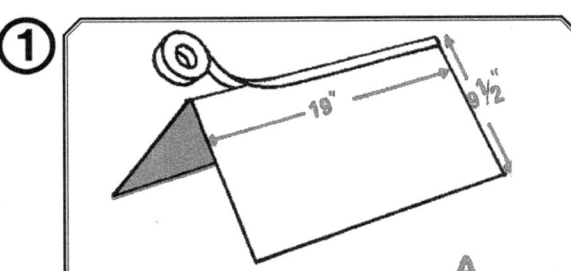
Take thick cards 19" X 9 ½" and join together with tape. Leave ⬜" between to allow pieces to bend easily.

②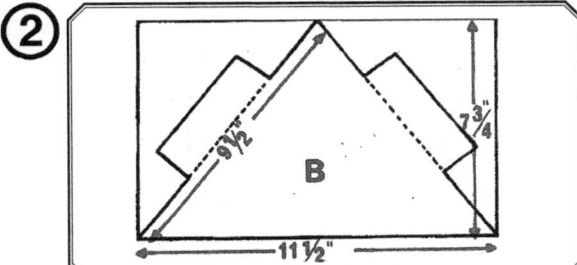
Draw 2 sections as above on thick card 7 ¾ " X 11 ½". Cut and fold as shown. These are for roof supports.

③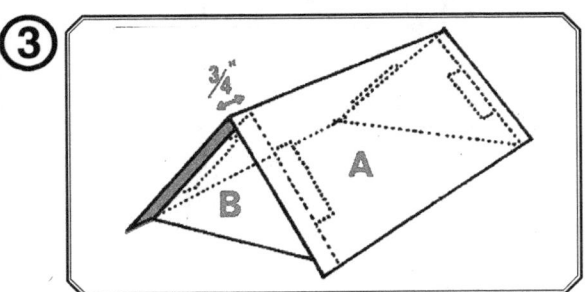
Glue roof supports B into roof top A. Leave ¾" overlap at each end of roof.

④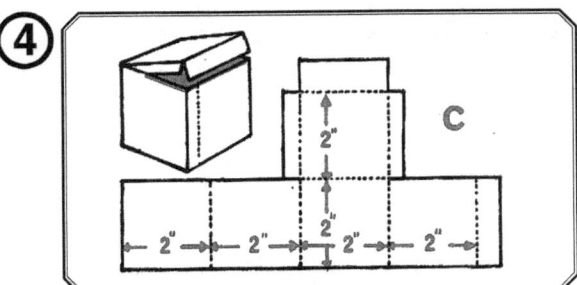
Draw and cut 2 sections as above from thin cards 8 ½" X 4 ½". Fold and glue tabs to make chimney stacks.

⑤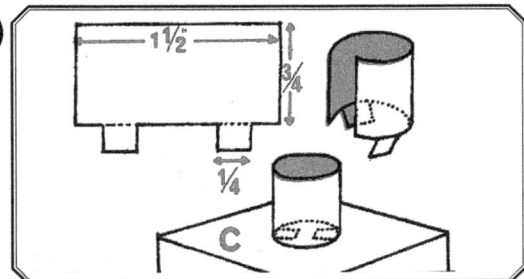
Draw and cut pattern for two chimney pots from thin card 1 ½ X 1". Roll and glue edge. Glue tabs onto stacks.

⑥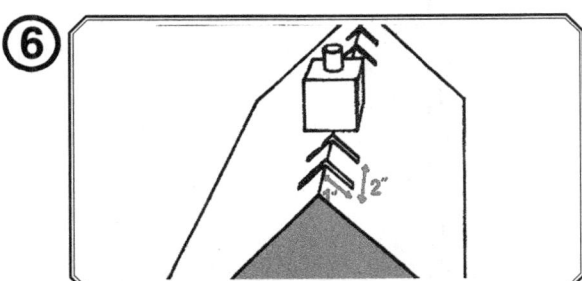
Cut a pair of slots 2" apart and 1" deep at each end of the roof top. Fit chimney stacks into slots.

⑦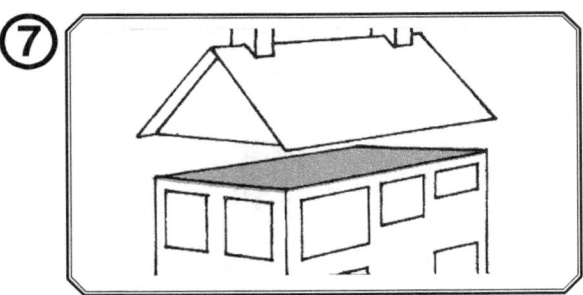
Place the roof on the house.

⑧
Decorate the roof and chimneys with coloured paints to complete the exterior of the house.

10
Softy Soft Toy

Materials Required

* Two pieces of coloured felt 9" × 5"
* Piece of coloured felt 11½ × 3"
* Triangle piece of felt 2½" × 3"
* Triangular piece of felt 5" × 3"
* Four pieces of coloured felt 3" × 5"
* Strip of felt 12" × 1"
* Scarps of coloured felt
* Cotton wool
* Scissors needle and thread

①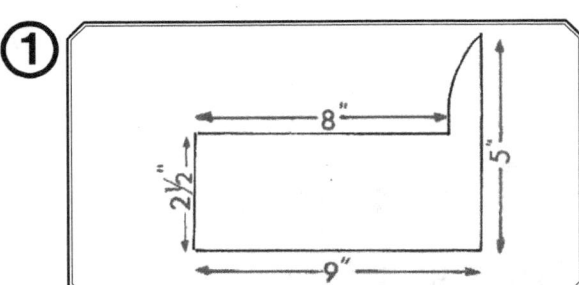
Draw and cut the above pattern twice for sides of body.

⑤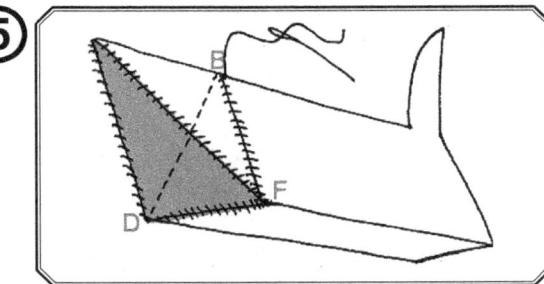
Stitch these sections together to form pyramid and sew to body at BFD.

②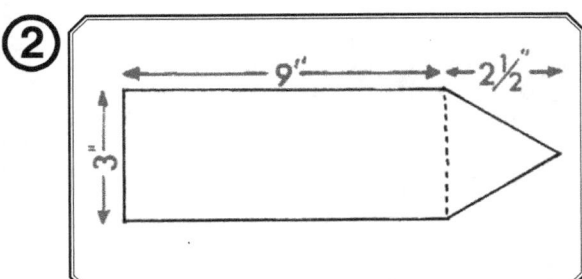
Draw and cut pattern for base of soft toy.

⑥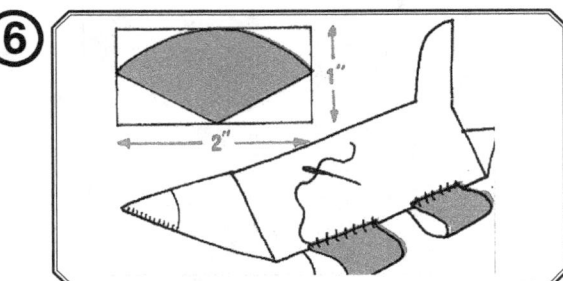
Fold over 4 pieces of felt 3" X 5", and stitch to body for paws. Cut pattern for nose and stitch to face.

③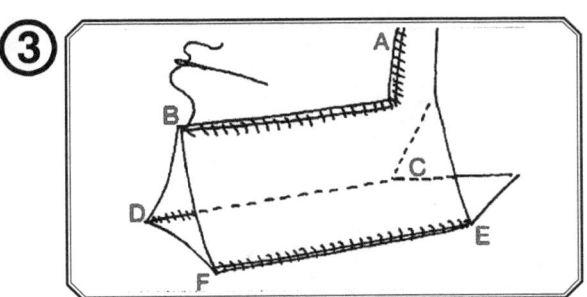
Sew two sides together from A to B. Sew sides to base along EF and CD.

⑦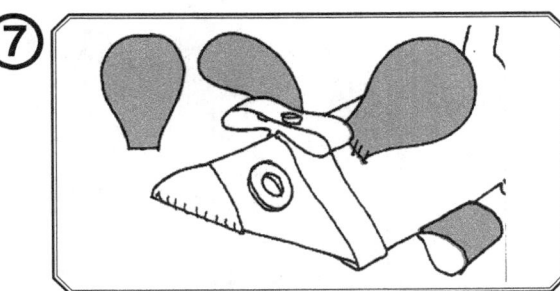
Draw and cut patterns for eyes and ears. Sew to body. Take strip 12" X 1", Stitch around neck and form into bow.

④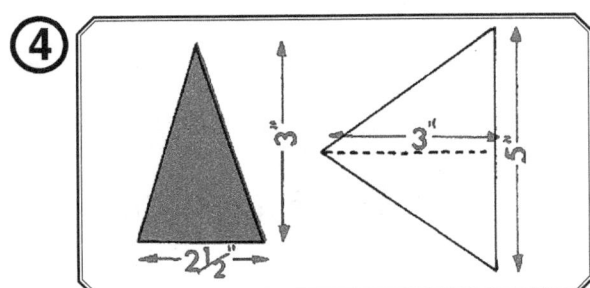
Cut two triangular patterns shown above from felt for head.

⑧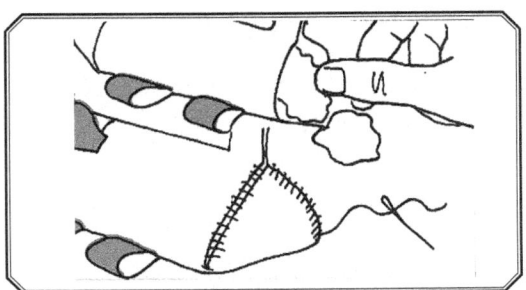
Stuff toy from tail end with cotton wool and sew up back flap. Now your soft toy is complete.

11

"Snakey" the Draught Excluder and Desk Tidy

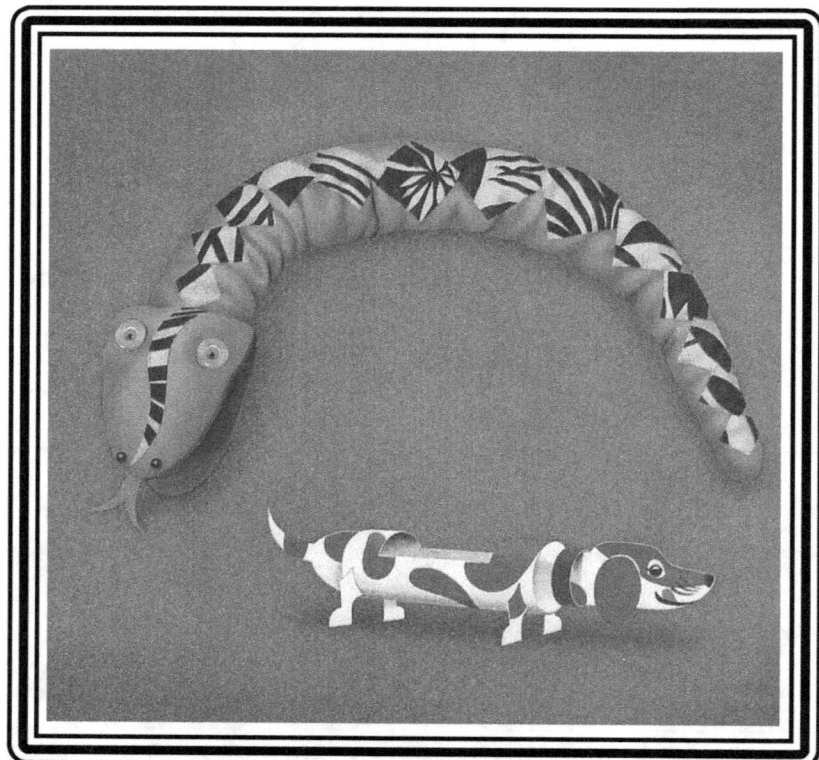

Materials Required

'Snakey' the Draft Excluder

* Piece of cloth 36" long × 12" wide
* Four pieces of cloth 9" long × 6" Wide (different colours)
* Rags for stuffing
* Two buttons
* Scraps of coloured cloth
* Scissors, needle and thread

Desk Tidy

* Plastic detergent bottle
* Thee pieces of thick card 3½" square
* Piece of thick card 5½" square for head
* Glue
* Pencil, scissors, good penknife, coloured paints

'Snakey' the Draft Excluder

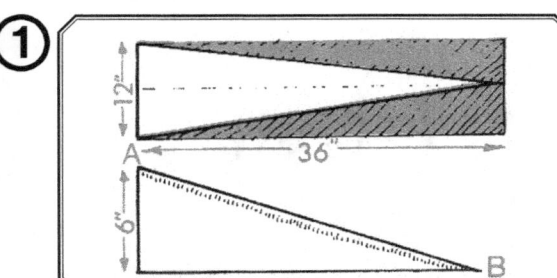

① Cut out pattern for body, as shown. Fold and sew from A to B. Then turn inside out.

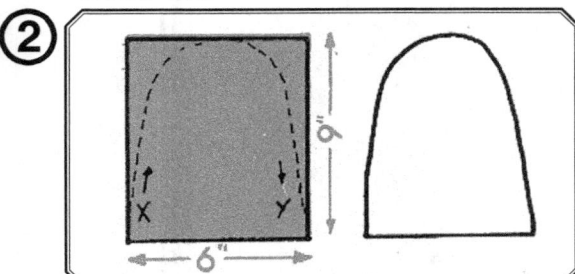

② Cut 9" X 6" piece to pattern. Sew two pieces together. Repeat, and turn both inside out. These are the head pieces.

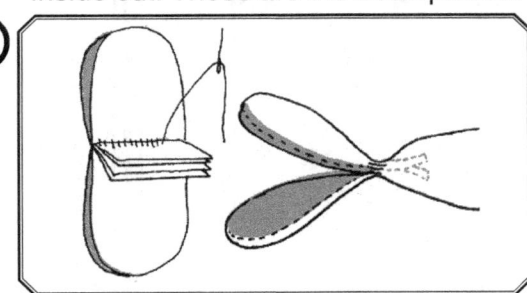

③ Stuff body and head pieces with rags. Then sew head pieces together, insert head flaps into body and stitch across neck.

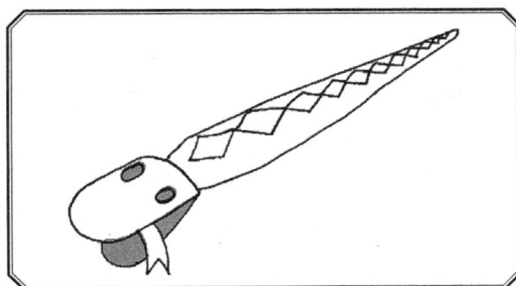

④ Sew on bottoms for eyes, and other scraps of coloured cloth for decoration.

Desk Tidy

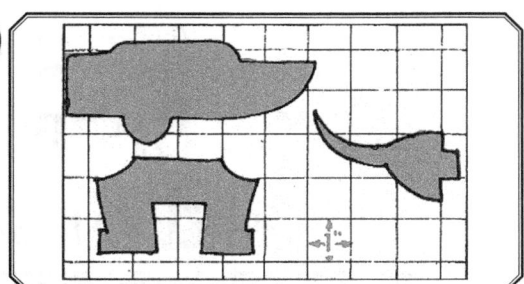

① Draw and cut patterns on cards for legs, head and tail. Cut section from one side of bottle as shown below.

② Cut slots in sides of bottle for legs and in top and bottom for head and tail. Glue on legs as shown.

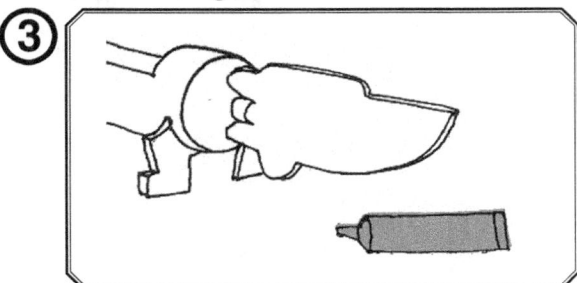

③ Push head into top and secure with glue.

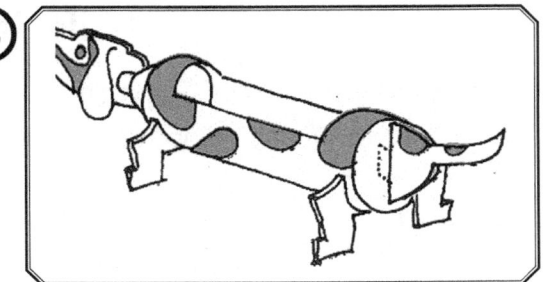

④ Push tail into bottom of bottle. Paint your holder and fill it with pencils.

12

Three Dimensional Picture and Mosaic Picture

Materials Required

Three Dimensional Picture

* Piece of thick cardboard 20" × 14"
* Old boxes, tins, pieces of wood, etc
* Strong glue
* Coloured paint

Mosaic Pictures

* Coloured magazines
* Piece of thin card 10" × 8"
* Scissors
* Eraser
* Pencil
* Glue

Three Dimensional Picture

①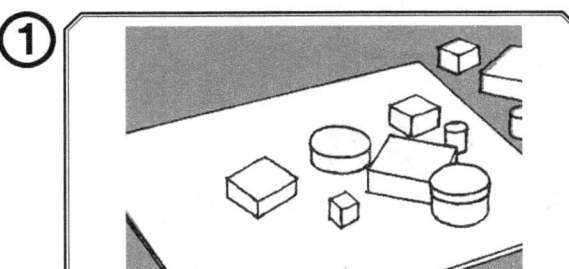

Put the board on a flat surface. Put the scraps of wood, boxes and tins on the board.

②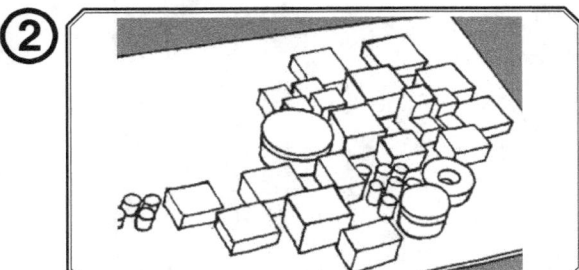

Move them around until they form an interesting pattern.

③

Now glue each piece in position.

④

Choose a bright colour and paint the base and the pieces. Paint the tops of some shapes a different colour.

Mosaic Pictures

①

Lightly draw the outline for your picture in pencil on a piece of thin card 10" X 8".

②

Remove coloured pictures from magazines and cut them into ½" squares.

③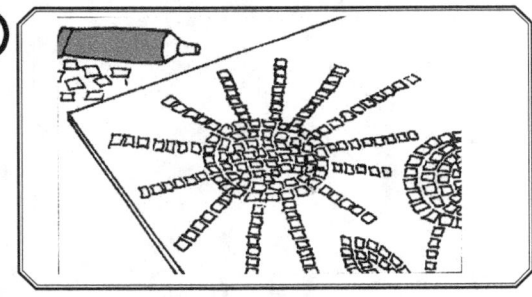

Group the pieces into colours and begin sticking them onto your picture until each shape is filled in.

④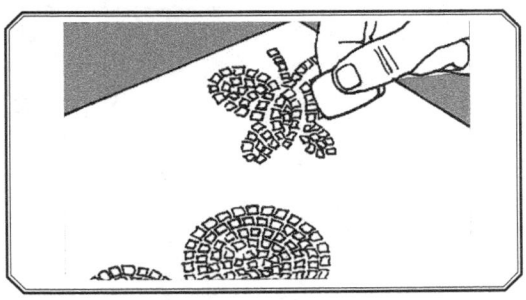

Erase the pencil outline to complete your mosaic picture.

13
Clown Stick Puppet

Materials Required

- Paper disc 2" diameter
- Half-circle of thin card 12" diameter
- Round stick 18" long
- Cloth 12" x 8"
- Table tennis ball
- Wool
- Glue and Cellotape
- Length of ribbon, scissors
- Needle and thread
- Coloured paints

①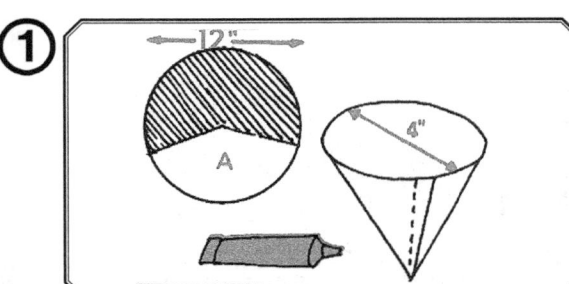
Cut segment A from your thin card and glue to make cone 4" diameter.

②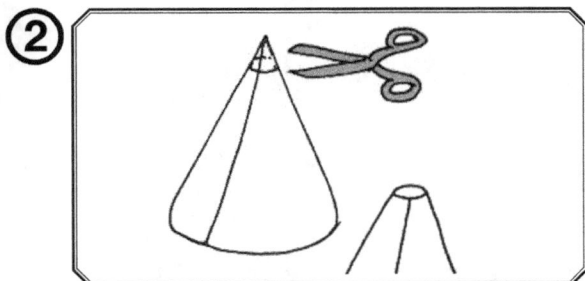
Cut off the point of the cone to make a hole for the stick.

③
Fold cloth in half. Mark and stitch around shape as shown to make costume.

④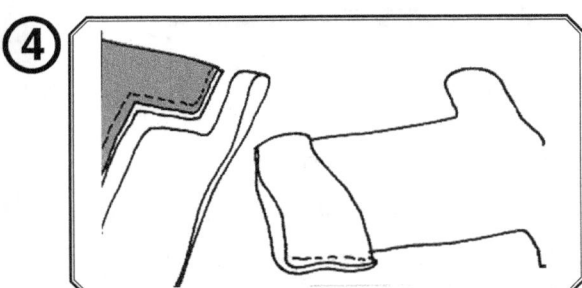
Cut away the cloth outside the stitches. Then turn the costume inside out.

⑤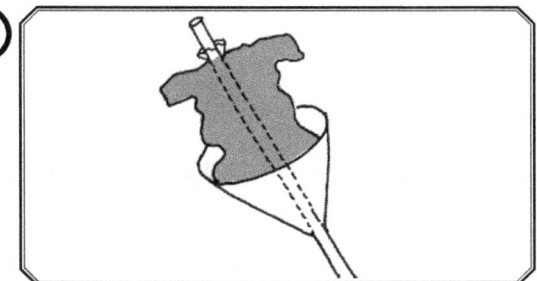
Cut a small hole in the top of the costume and push stick through cone and costume.

⑥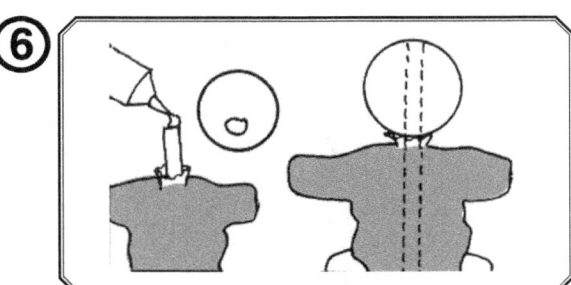
Make a hole in the table tennis ball. Insert the stick and glue it on as shown.

⑦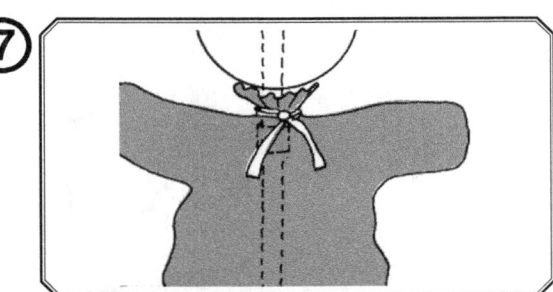
Wrap tape around stick as shown. Then tie costume tightly to stick just above the tape to stop it slipping.

⑧
Stitch bottom of costume to edge of cone. Make collar from 2" paper disc, glue on wool for hair and paint face.

14

Garden Landscape (Part 3)

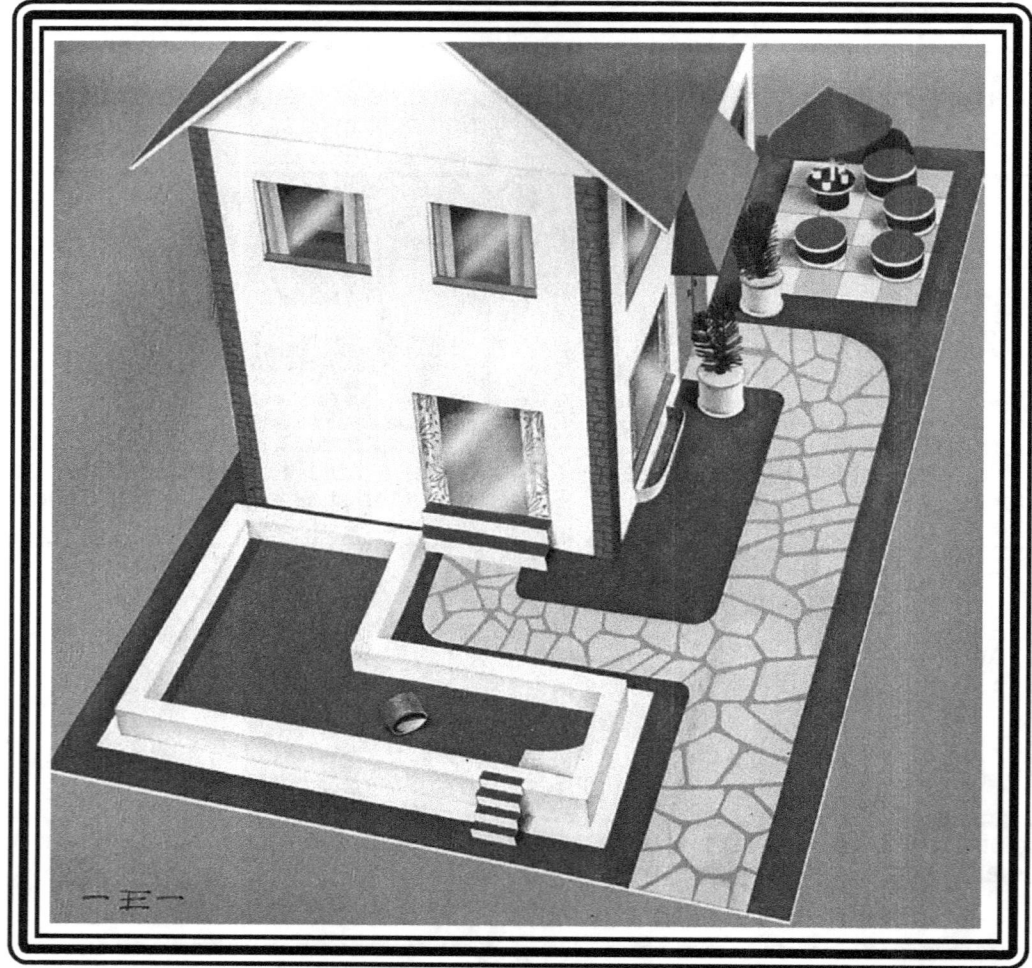

Materials Required

- Coloured paper 4½" square
- Coloured paper for path
- Thin card 8" × 4"
- Thin card 5" × 4"
- Two cotton reels
- Two small twigs
- Egg carton lid or paper tray
- Glue, scissors, pencil, ruler
- Coloured paints

①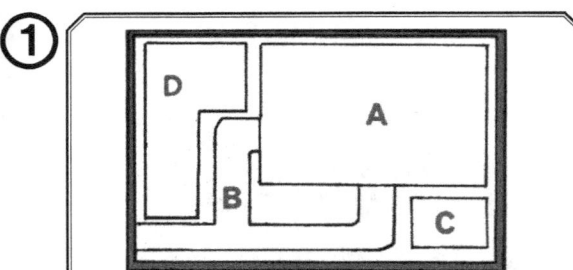
Draw out the plan on your base in pencil. A is the house; B path; C patio and D pool.

⑤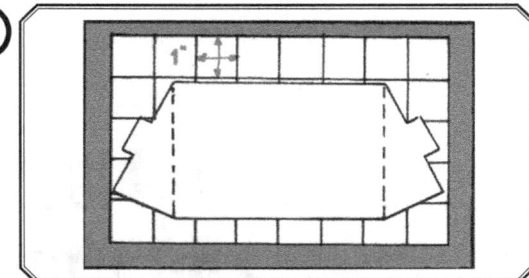
Draw and cut paper pattern for canopy over door. Fold and glue over door.

②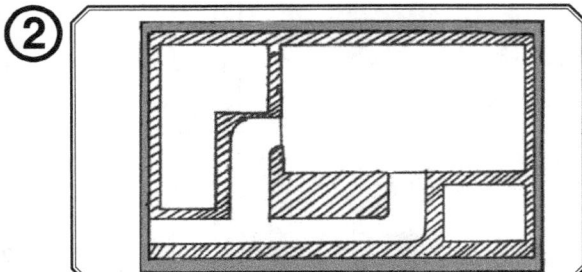
Paint the shaded areas green.

⑥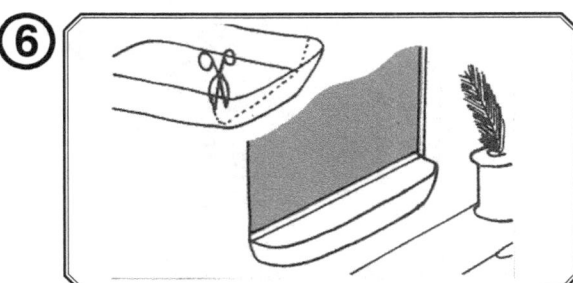
Cut an egg carton lid or paper tray to make window box. Glue below window.

③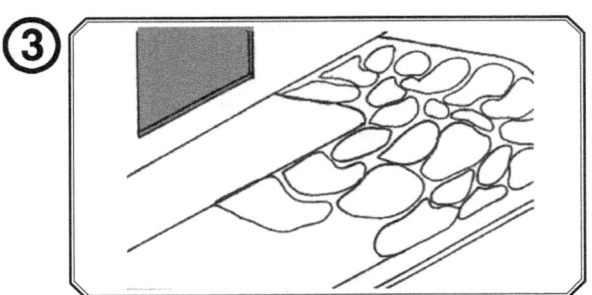
Cut irregular shapes in grey or brown paper and glue them to the paths.

⑦
Cut twenty 1" squares from 5" X 4" card. Glue them on the base to make patio (C).

④
Cut and glue on 2 pieces of coloured paper 2¼" X 4½" from paper 4½" square, for front doors. Paint on door-knobs.

⑧
Paint 2 reels white and put them at either side of the front door, with a small twig in each.

15

Outdoor Noughts & Crosses and Whipping Top

Materials Required

Outdoor Noughts & Crosses
* Four strips of thick card 36" × 1"
* Five piece of card 9" square
* Five discs of card 9" diameter
* Scissors, good penknife

Whipping Top
* Cotton reel
* 3" disc of heavy card
* Pencil 3" long
* 10" piece of dowel
* 12" of thin string
* Glue
* Penknife

Outdoor Noughts & Crosses

①
Cut out pattern from five pieces of square card to make your crosses.

②
Cut centre out of discs as shown to make the noughts for your game.

③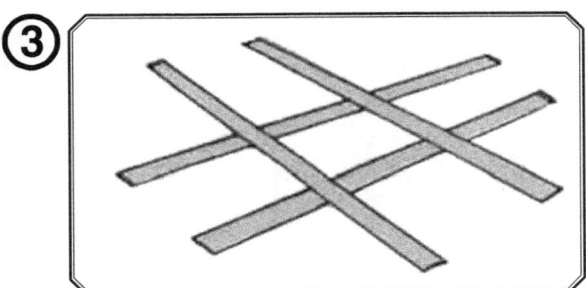
Lay out the strips as shown to make the grid.

④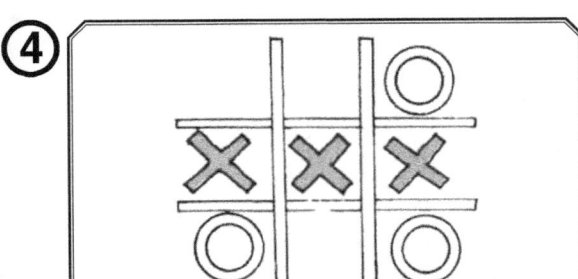
Ask a friend to join you. Begin placing the noughts and crosses onto grid. First to get 3 in a row wins.

Whipping Top

①
Make hole in centre of disc and glue reel to it so that holes correspond.

②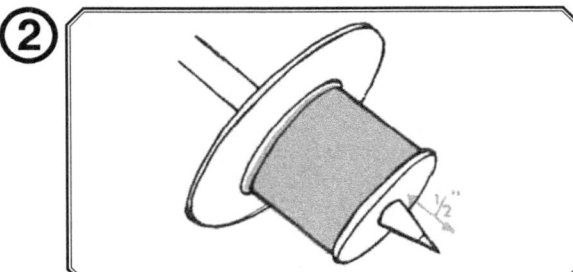
Push pencil through reel and disc. Glue it in position with ½" protruding at pointed end.

③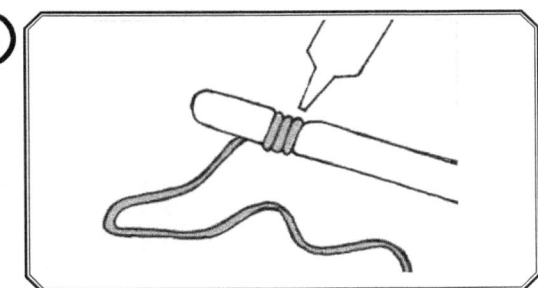
Cut a notch in the end of the dowel with a penknife. Tie and glue string to it.

④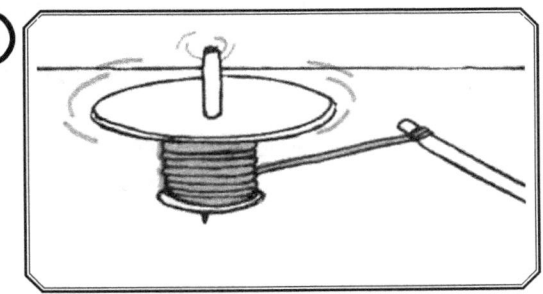
Wind string around the reel. Place top on floor. Pull string off with a twist and watch it spin.

16

Table Decoration

Materials Required

- Plastic detergent bottle
- Piece of thick card 12" × 10"
- Three discs of white paper
- 10" diameter
- Glass tumbler
- Candle
- Tin foil
- Glue and Cellotape
- Scissors, good penknife
- Green paint

①
Draw and cut pattern for leaf base from thick card 12" X 10"

②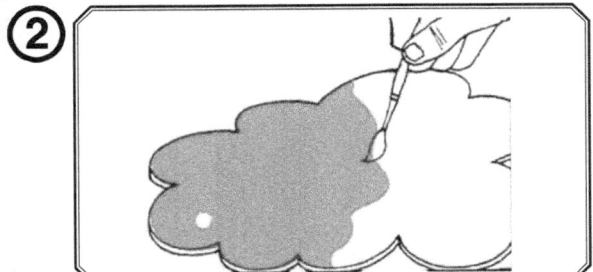
Paint the leaf base green and leave to dry.

③
Draw and cut pattern above from three 10" diameter discs of white paper. Curl up the ends of petal, as shown.

④
Arrange and glue the 3 petal shapes together to make the finished flower. Glue them to centre of leaf base.

⑤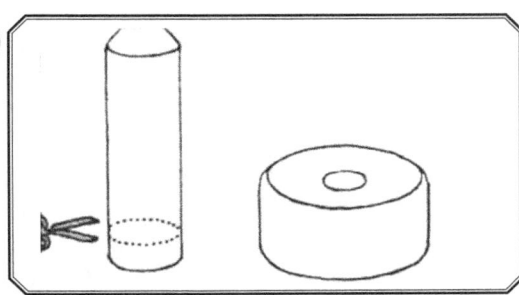
Cut the base from a plastic bottle 1" from the bottom for holder. Make hole in it to fit candle.

⑥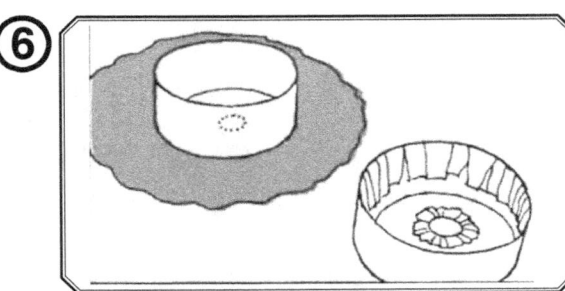
Cover the holder in tin foil and glue overlap inside.

⑦
Glue holder inside glass tumbler. Stand tumbler in centre of flower, as shown.

⑧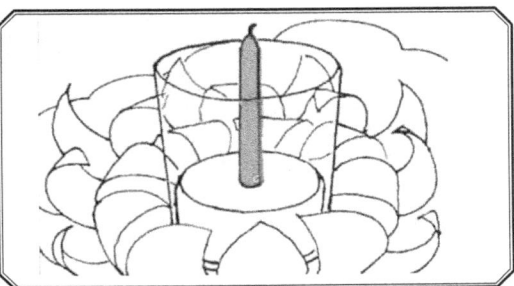
Push a candle into the holder and place your decoration in the centre of the table.

17

'Lace' Picture Frame and Felt Pictures

Materials Required

'Lace' Picture Frame
* A picture or photograph
* A much larger piece of
* Coloured paper
* Paper doilies
* Paste
* Scissors

Felt Pictures
* A piece of white cardboard
* Scraps of coloured felt or cloth
* Glue
* Pencil
* Scissors

'Lace' Picture Frame

①

Take your favourite picture or photograph from a magazine and cut it out.

②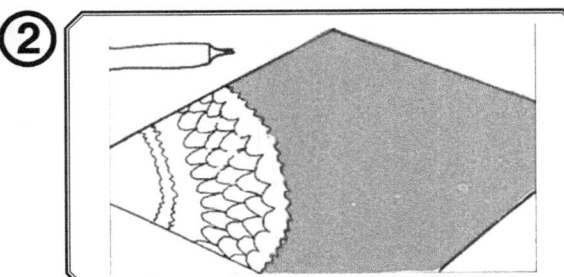

Fold and cut a paper doily into four equal parts. Paste these in corners of coloured paper.

③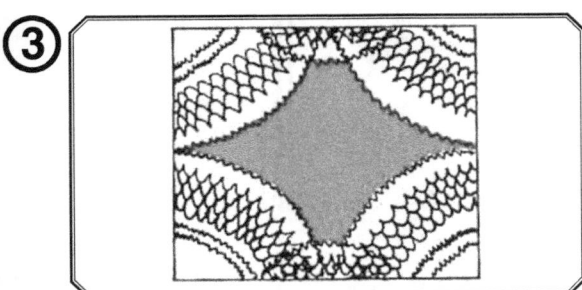

Cut pieces from other doilies to complete edge of frame.

④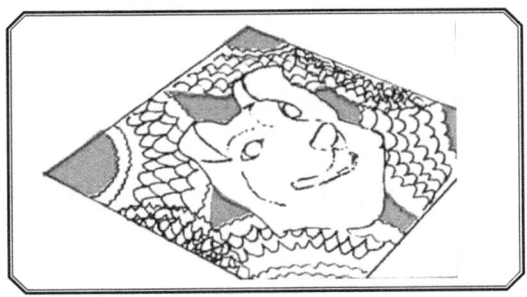

Take your picture and paste it in the middle of your 'lace' frame.

Felt Pictures

①

Your first felt picture could be an owl. Draw him on the cardboard like this.

②

Cut the coloured felt into shapes to match the different parts of your drawing.

③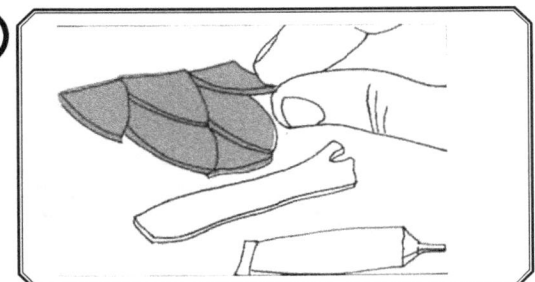

Stick on the feathers, beginning at the bottom, until you reach the head.

④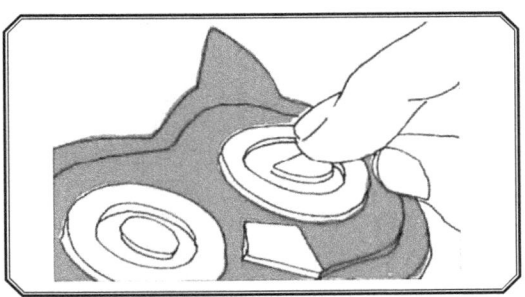

Stick on the head. Use circles for eyes. Try making more felt pictures of different animals.

18

Sock-Head Clown and Puppet Theatre

Materials Required

Sock-Head Clown
* An old sock
* Cotton wool
* Ribbon
* Cloth 14" × 7"
* Wool
* Scraps of cloth
* Glue
* Thin string
* Scissors, coloured paints
* Stick 5" long
* Needle and thread

Puppet Theatre
* Large carton or cardboard box 24" × 12" × 19"
* Two pieces of cloth
* Piece of string
* Scissors, needle and thread
* Coloured paints or crayons

Sock-Head Clown

①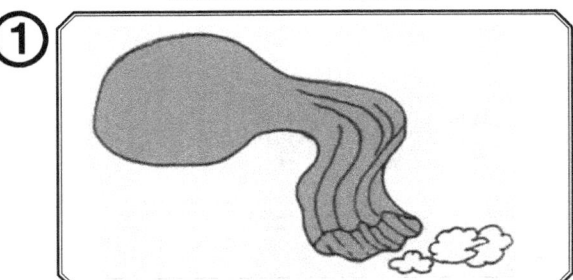

Stuff cotton wool into the toe of an old sock to make a head for your clown.

②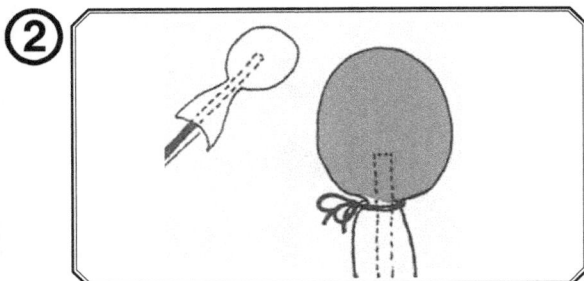

Push stick into centre and tie string tightly round the base of the head and make a knot.

③

Fold cloth in half and sew. Cut off excess cloth and cut hole at top. Turn inside out.

④

Tie costume to neck with ribbon. Glue on scraps of cloth to make the eyes, nose and mouth. Use wool for hair.

Puppet Theatre

①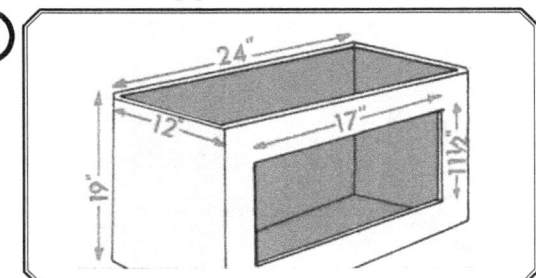

Cut off the top of your carton, then cut a large opening in the front, as shown

②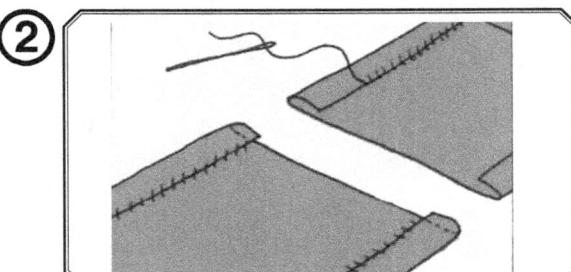

Cut pieces of cloth to fit opening. Fold over the top and bottom of the pieces and sew to make curtains.

③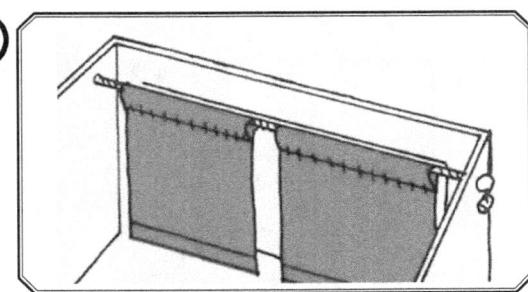

Make holes at the sides of the box. Thread string through the curtains. Fasten them across the stage opening.

④

Cut panel out of back leaving 2" strip across top. Open the curtains and your show can begin.

Garden Furniture and Pool (Part 4)

Materials Required

* Sheet of thin coloured card
* Toilet roll tube
* Cotton reel
* Lolly stick
* Pieces of thin card for sides of pool : 12" × 4", 8" × 4", 7" × 4", 5" ×4" and two 4" squares
* Glue
* Pencil, scissors, coloured paints

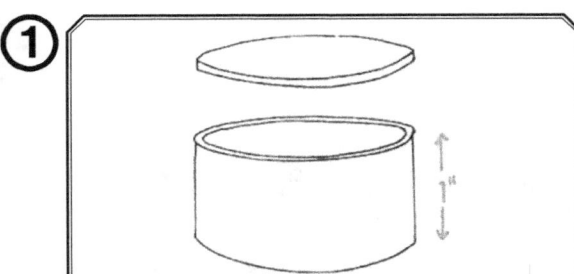

Cut four 1" lengths from toilet roll tube. Cut four discs from card to fit the tops and glue into place for chairs.

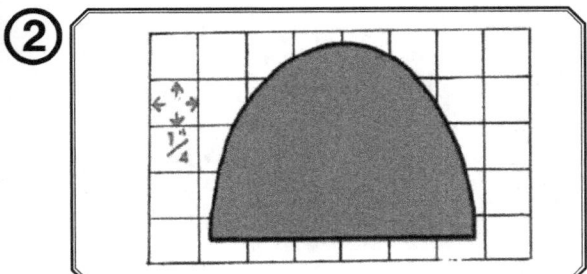

Draw and cut pattern for seat back from card and glue to one seat.

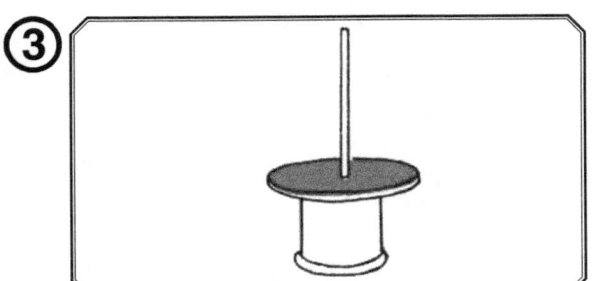

For the table glue a 1 ½" disc of card to top of cotton reel. Push the stick through the centre.

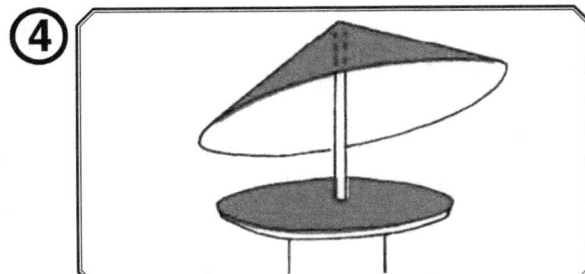

Make sunshade from a 4 ½" disc of paper. Cut and glue into cone. Fix on top of stick as shown.

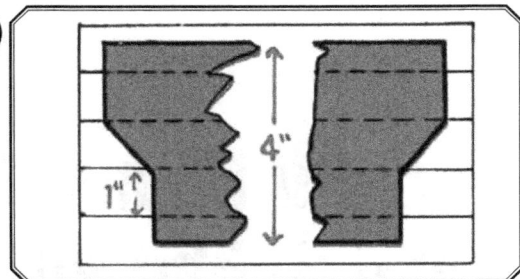

Draw and cut out above shapes at each end of the cards for sides of pool. Fold along dotted lines.

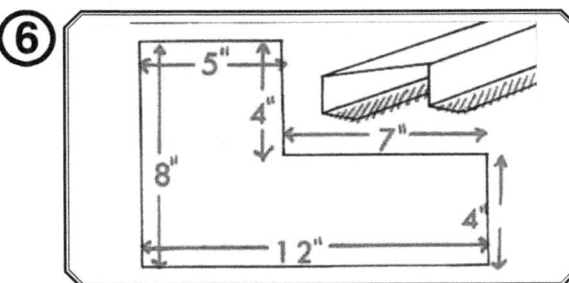

Glue into position around pool, following the above plan. Paint bottom of the pool blue.

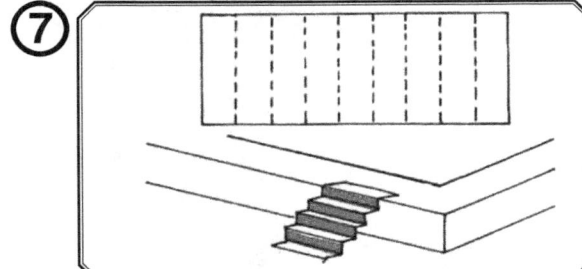

Make steeps from card 2 ½" X 1". Fold at every ¼" as shown and glue into place.

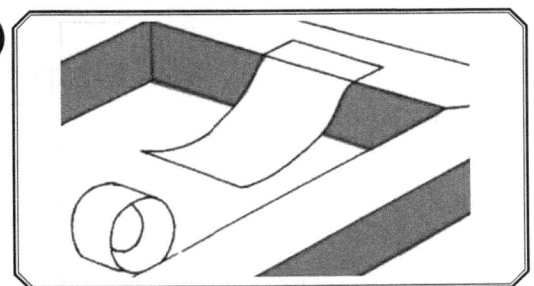

Cut two 2" X 1" strips of card. Curve one for chute and make other into tube for decoration. Glue both to pool.

20

Potato Man with Hair that Grow and Rabbit with Ears that Grow

Materials Required

Potato Man with Hair that Grow
* One large Potato
* Packet of cress seeds
* Cotton Wool
* Good penknife
* Coloured paints, water

Rabbit with Ears that Grow
* Four fresh carrot tops
* Empty tin can
* Enough small stones to almost fill can
* Coloured paints, water

Potato Man with Hair that Grow

①
Cut off the top and bottom of your potato.

②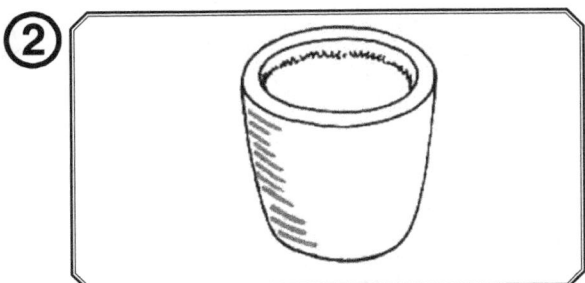
Scoop out the top to leave hole about 1" deep. Fill hole with damp cotton wool.

③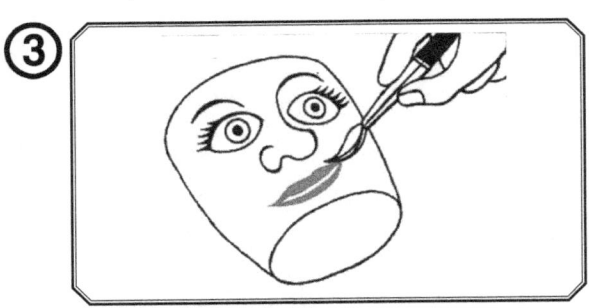
Carefully paint a face on the potato

④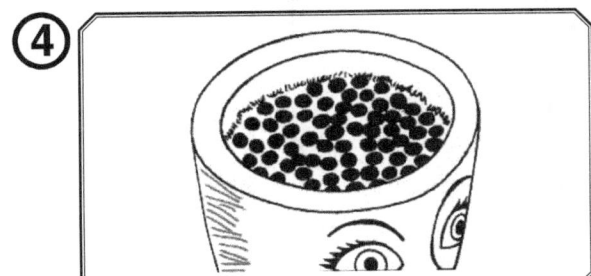
Sprinkle the cress seeds on top of the cotton wool and wait for the hair to grow. Remember to keep the cotton wool moist.

Rabbit with Ears that Grow

①
Decorate small tin as shown, with rabbit's face.

②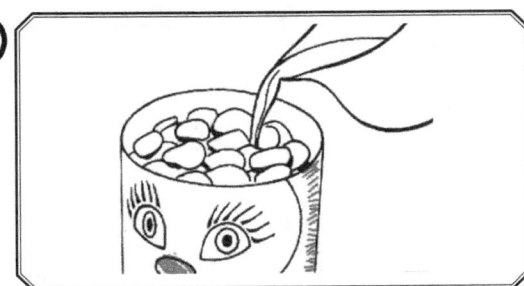
Put the small stones in the tin and fill with water.

③
Put two carrot tops on the stones at one side of the tin and two more on the other side.

④
Hold the base of each ear down with stones then watch your rabbit's ears grow. Make sure you keep them well watered.

21

Montage Picture Calendar and Pop-Up Card

Materials Required

Montage Picture Calendar
* Piece of coloured cardboard 18" × 15"
* Piece of paper 14" × 10"
* Scraps of coloured paper
* Calendar
* Glue
* Scissors, pencil

Pop-Up Card
* Piece of card 16" × 10"
* Pencil, good penknife,
* coloured paints

Montage Picture Calendar

①
Draw and cut out shapes from coloured paper as shown.

②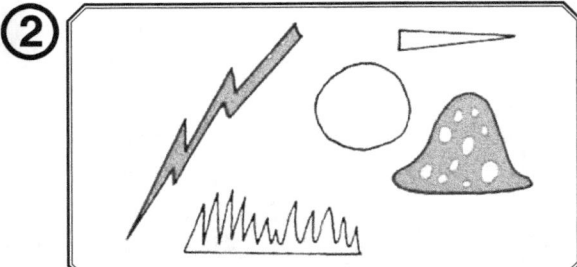
Cut out some more shapes, in different colours.

③
Arrange them in group, and glue them onto the paper.

④
When your picture is finished, glue paper onto card and glue calendar underneath. Attach string to hang it up.

Pop-Up Card

①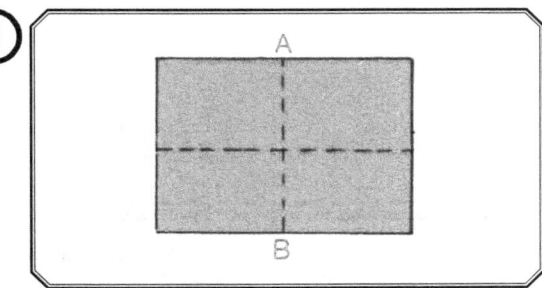
Fold card in half, along line A to B.

②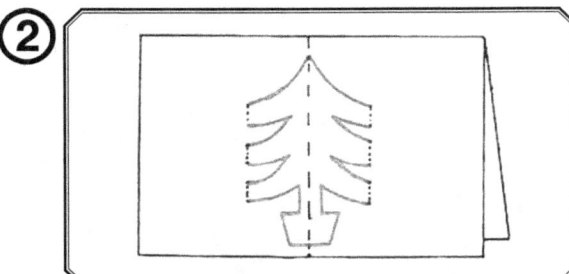
Draw tree in centre of card. Cut along red lines – but leave the ends of branches uncut.

③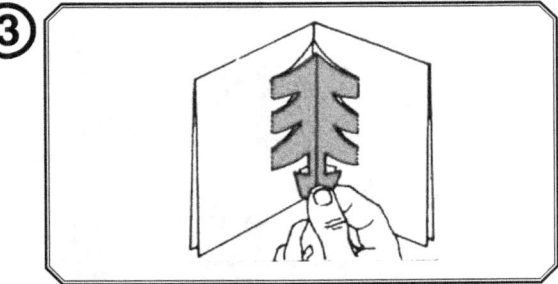
Push Christmas tree towards you, and fold the centre crease the other way. Now close the card.

④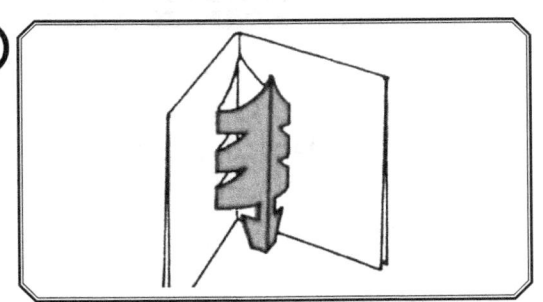
Paint and decorate the tree. Write on the words 'Merry Christmas' and a Christmas message.

22
Collage Picture

Materials Required

- Sheet of paper or card
- Wool
- Cloth
- Cotton wool
- Coloured paper
- Pipe cleaners
- Straw
- Small flowers or petals
- Grass
- Small leaves
- Glue
- Pencil, scissors

①
Draw a picture on the paper as a pattern.

②
Cut cloth to make clothes, coloured paper for house, ladder, cart etc.

③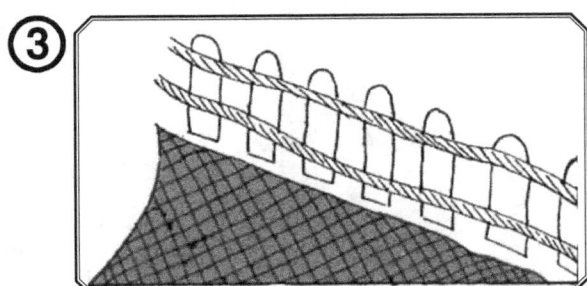
Make fence with paper and wool, and stick onto your drawing. Stick on green cloth for field.

④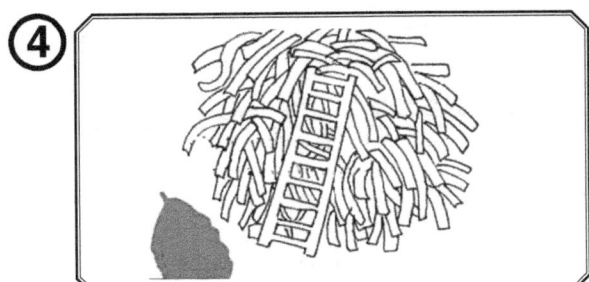
Use straw for the haystacks and glue on the ladder.

⑤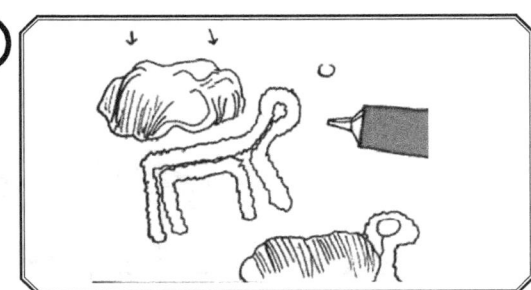
Make sheep by gluing cotton wool onto pipe cleaner shape, as shown.

⑥
Make the scarecrow as shown, and glue him in the field.

⑦
Glue on large pieces of paper for house. Use smaller pieces for windows, doors and chimney.

⑧
Stick on the flowers, leaves, cotton wool clouds and grass until your collage picture is complete.

23
Girl Dress-Up Doll

Materials Required

* Piece of thick cardboard 1 ft. square
* Plain paper for doll's clothes
* Scissors, coloured paints

①
Draw and cut out patterns for doll and base. Fit slots together and stand her up.

②
Paint girl's hands, legs, face and underclothes.

③
Draw and cut out pattern for coat. Decorate it. Bend tabs and place on doll's shoulders.

④
Draw and cut out pattern for dress and decorate. Dress the doll as before.

⑤
Draw and cut out pattern for winter sports outfit. Decorate and dress doll.

⑥
Draw and cut out pattern for sweater. Decorate. Place it over the dress.

⑦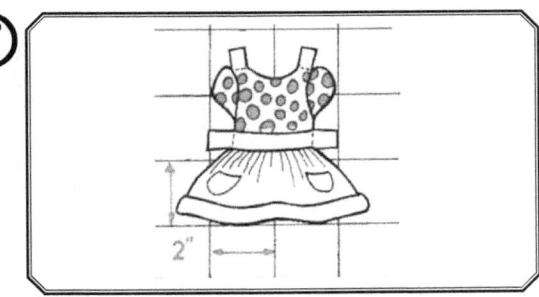
Draw and cut out pattern for party dress. Decorate. Place over as before.

⑧
Draw and cut out patterns for skirt and shoes. Decorate, bend tabs around waist and ankles.

24
Lounge Furniture (Part 5)

Materials Required

- Egg box carton lid
- Thin coloured card
- Stiff coloured paper
- Tin foil 3½" × 1 ½"
- Scissors, glue, ruler
- coloured paints
- Pencil

①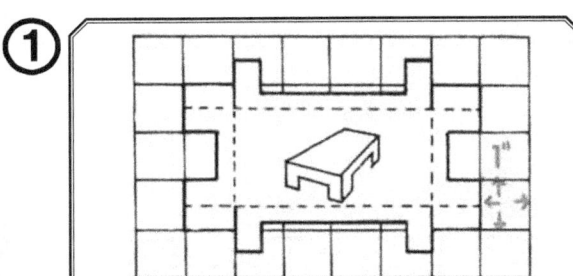
Draw pattern for table on card. Cut along solid lines, fold along dotted lines and glue together.

②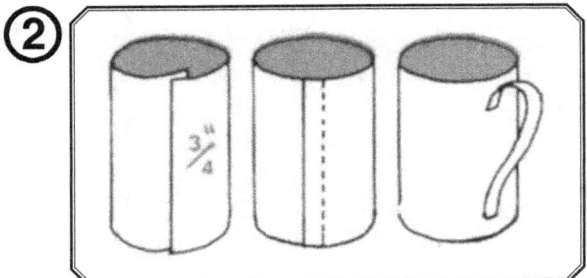
Cut a 1" X ¾" piece of card. Glue into a tube for jug. Stick on a thin strip of card for handle.

③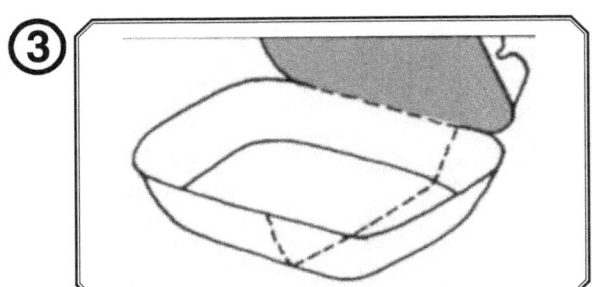
Cut an egg box lid as shown, to make couch.

④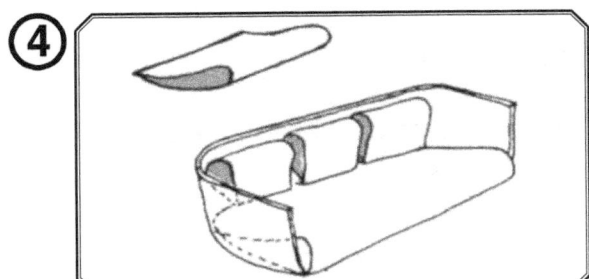
Cut and bend squares of paper for cushions. Glue to couch as shown. Use smaller squares for little cushions.

⑤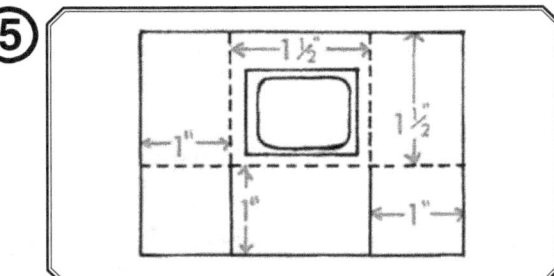
Draw pattern above on card for T.V. Cut along solid lines, fold along dotted lines and glue together to make a box.

⑥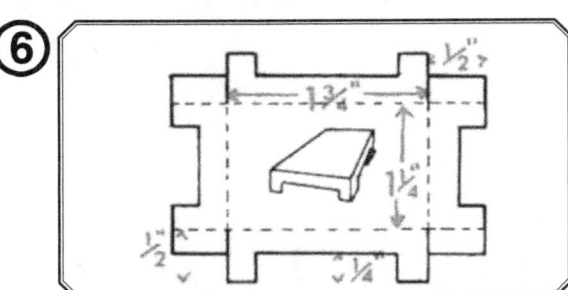
Draw and cut pattern for T.V. table from card. Fold along dotted lines and glue together. Decorate with paints.

⑦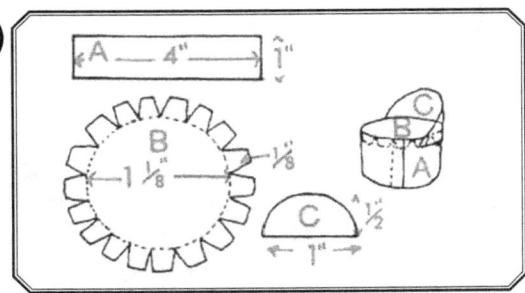
Draw and cut patterns for three seats from card. Roll 4" strips into tubes and glue on cushion and backs.

⑧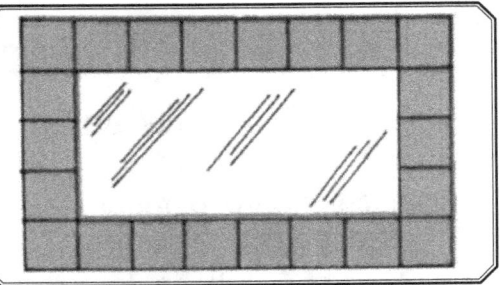
Cut card 4" x 2" for frame and glue a piece of foil 3 ½" x 1 ½" inside to make a mirror. Glue to wall.

25

Doll's Cradle

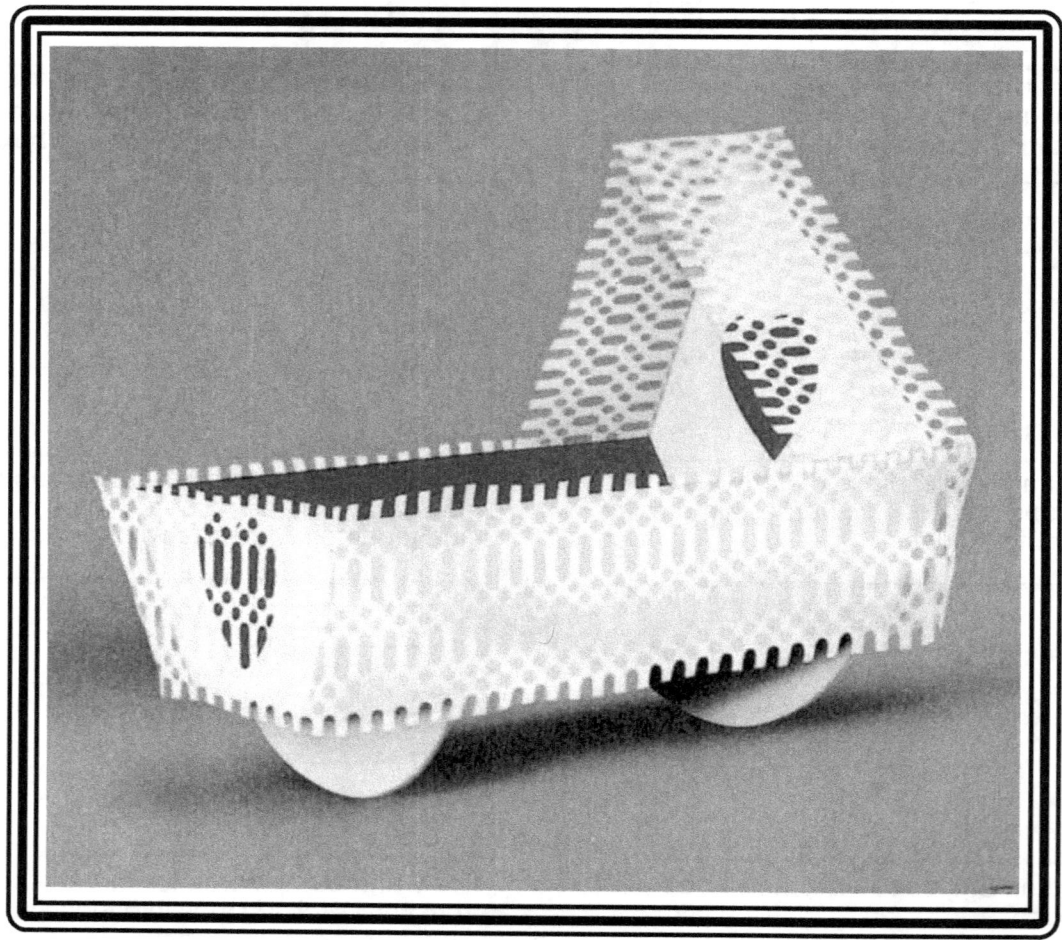

Materials Required

* Two piece of cardboard for rocker 7" × 2" (B) and (C)
* Piece of Cardboard for headboard 7½" × 8" (D)
* Piece of Cardboard for footboard 7½" × 5½" (E)
* Piece of Cardboard for base 9½" × 15" (A)
* Thick Wire
* Glue and Cellotape
* Pencil, Scissors
* Lace

①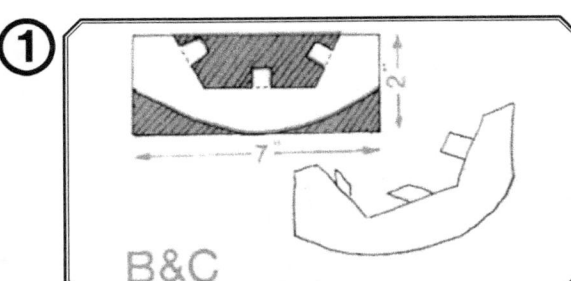
Cut two pieces of cardboard as shown to make cradle rockers.

②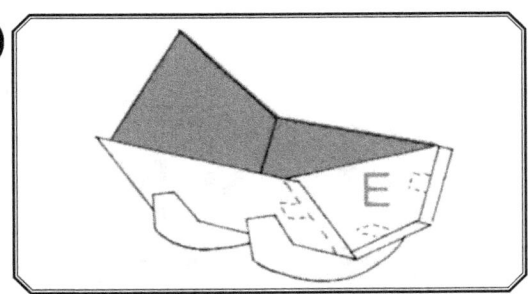
Cut the head and foot of the cradle as shown.

③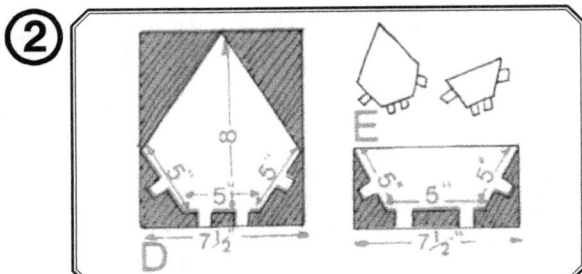
Fold piece of cardboard along dotted lines to make base and sides of cradle. Glue on the rockers.

④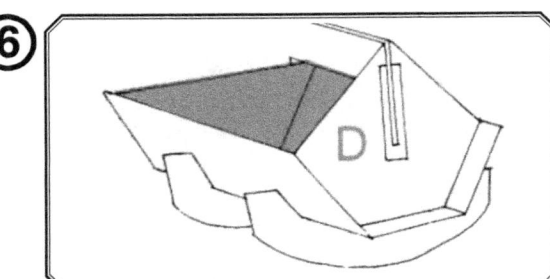
Fold tabs down, and glue on the head of the cradle to the base.

⑤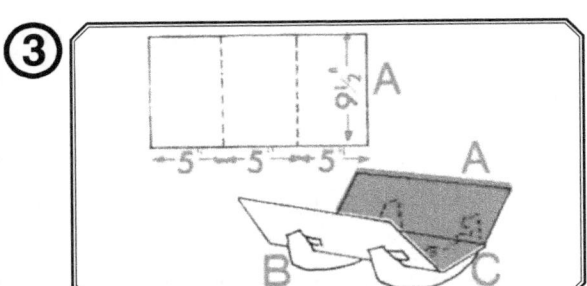
Now glue on the foot of the cradle in the same way.

⑥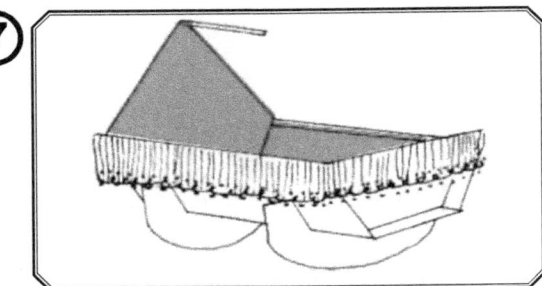
Bend wire to shape, and tape it onto headboard of cradle, as shown.

⑦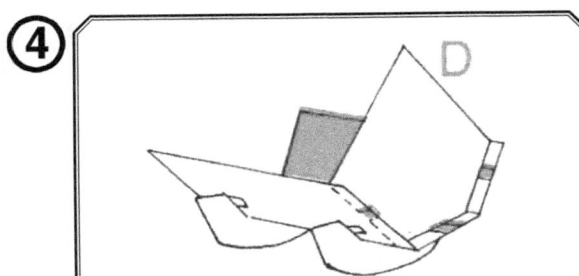
Glue strips of lace around the sides and foot of cradle.

⑧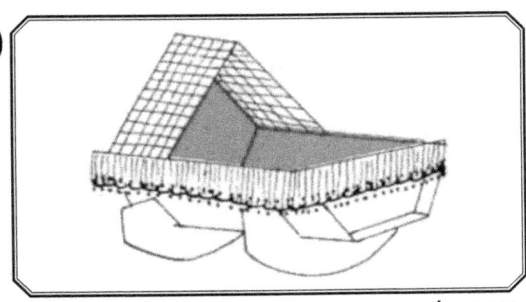
Glue on a lace canopy – and your doll's cradle is complete!

26

Paper Mats and Windmill

Materials Required

Paper Mats
* Two different coloured pieces of paper, one 14" × 10" the other 12" × 10"
* Glue
* Ruler
* Pencil
* Scissors

Windmill
* Coloured paper disc 8" diameter
* Twelve long strips for streamers ¼" wide
* ¼" dowel about 2 ft. long
* Wire about 6" long
* Disc of paper ¾" diameter
* Drinking straw
* Cellotape
* Pencil, Scissors, Pliers

Paper Mats

①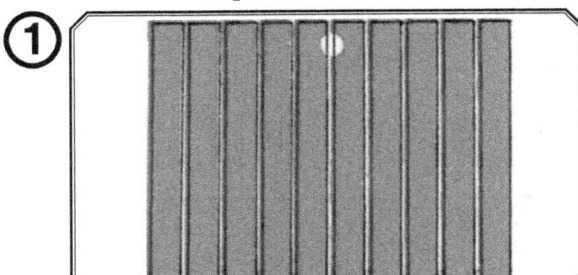

Draw and cut 10 pieces of coloured paper 1" wide by 14" long and 12 pieces 1" wide by 12" long.

②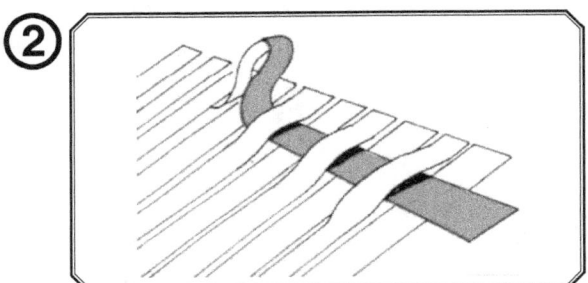

Weave the 14" strips between the 12" strips as shown.

③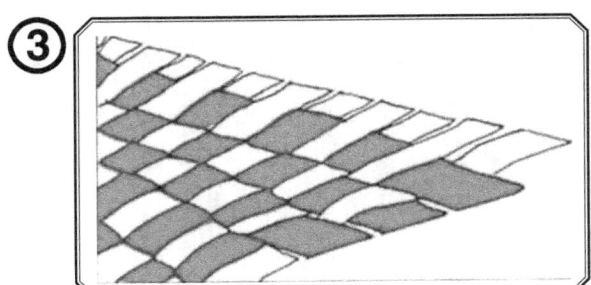

Carry on weaving until you have used all the strips.

④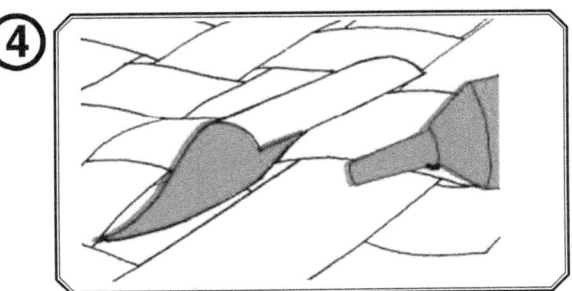

Then put a little glue where the strips meet at the end.

Windmill

①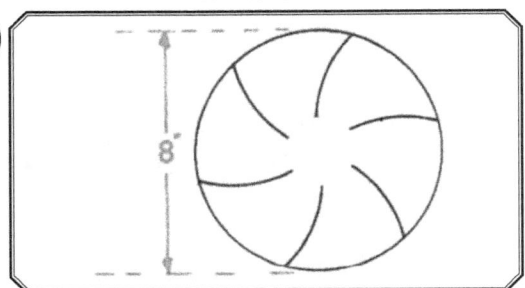

Draw and cut pattern as shown. Leave space in the centre.

②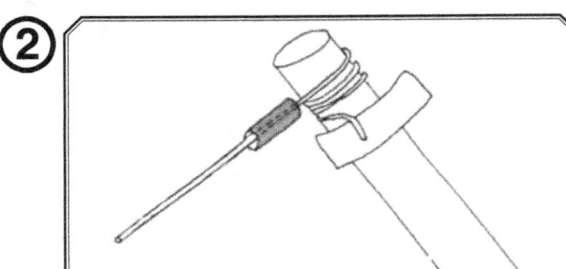

Bend wire as shown. Tape it to the stick. Cut ½" of drinking straw and fit over wire.

③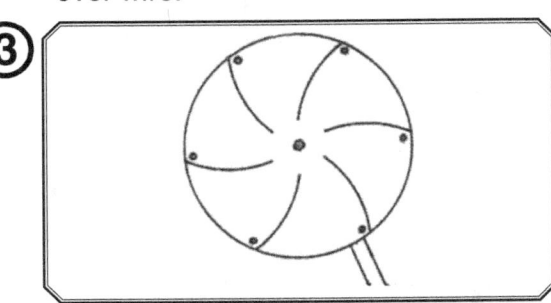

Make holes in the windmill as shown. Push end of wire through centre

④

Bend fins to centre and fit outside holes on wire. Add ¾" disc, then ½" straw and bend wire over. Tape streamers to stick.

27
Pom Pom Cat and French Knitting

Materials Required

Pom Pom Cat
* Ball of wool
* Two cardboard discs 3" diameter
* Scraps of coloured paper
* Thin string or thread
* Glue
* Scissors, darning needle

French Knitting
* Ball of wool
* Cotton reel
* Four nails ½" long with small heads
* Hammer, knitting needle

Pom Pom Cat

①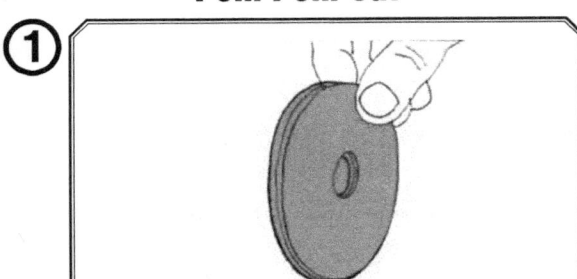
Cut ½" diameter holes in the centres of the cardboard discs.

②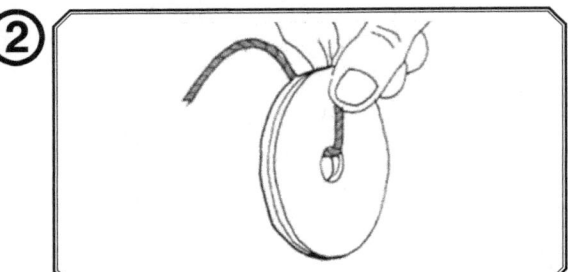
Hold the discs together. Push wool through centre holes, holding the ends together, as shown.

③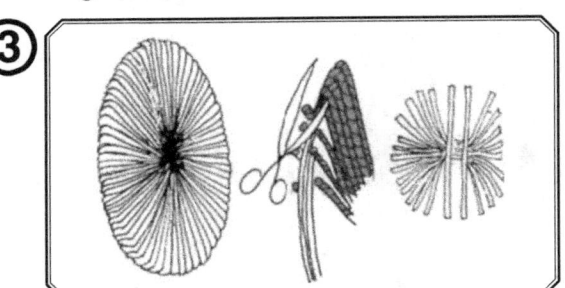
Wrap wool around the discs until full. Cut as shown, and tie tightly in centre before removing cards.

④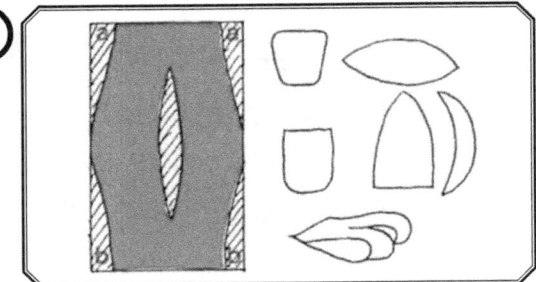
Cut above pattern and fold for paw. Add other shapes for eyes, nose, mouth, tongue and ears. Glue onto cat.

French Knitting

①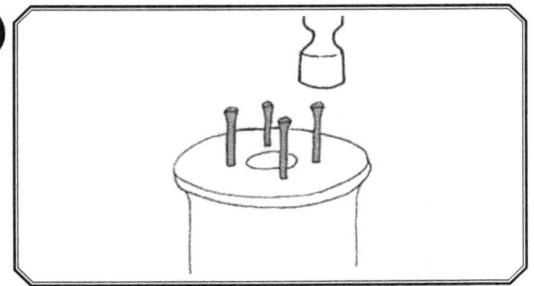
Hammer 4 nails into one end of cotton reel, as shown.

②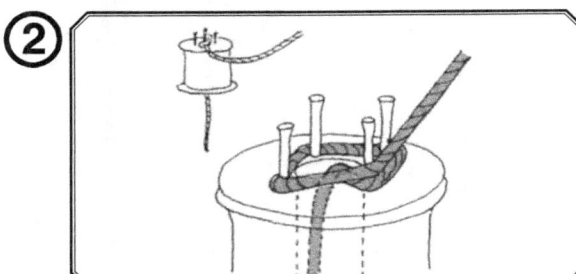
Push wool through hole in reel, then wind it around nails until you are back at first nail.

③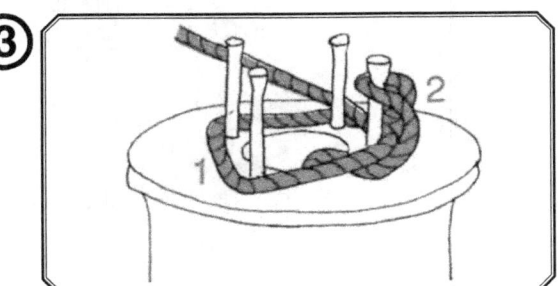
Lift bottom strand 2 over top strand 1. Loop it over nail with knitting needle.

④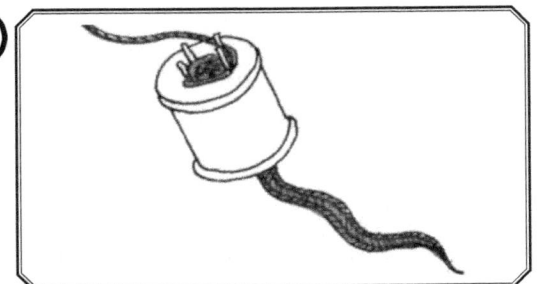
Continue doing this round the nails and see your French knitting come out at the bottom!

28
Rabbit and Witch Costumes

Materials Required

Rabbit
* Large sheets of stiff black paper
* Thin card 18" × 18"
* Black crepe paper
* String
* Strips of brown paper 12" long
* Piece of wood 36" long
* Two piece of cloth tape 12" long
* Pencil, scissors, cellotape

Witch
* Thin card 22" × 5"
* Thin card 27" × 18"
* Two discs of thin card, 10" diameter
* Paper sack or large sheet of brown paper
* Stiff paper 12" square for tail
* Glue, Cellotape
* Scissors, pencil, coloured paints

Rabbit

①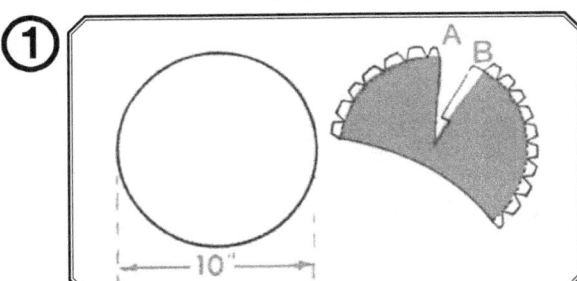
Cut the pattern shown from the two 10" card discs. Glue tab B to point A.

②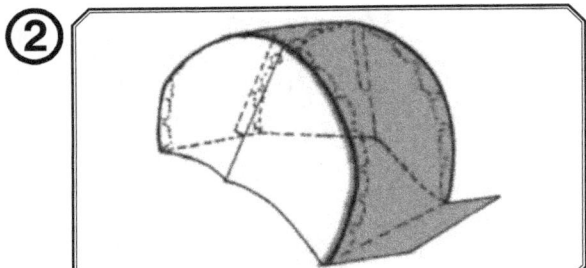
Bend disc tab inwards and glue to thin card 22" X 5" to form the cap. Fold back a flap at top edge of cap.

③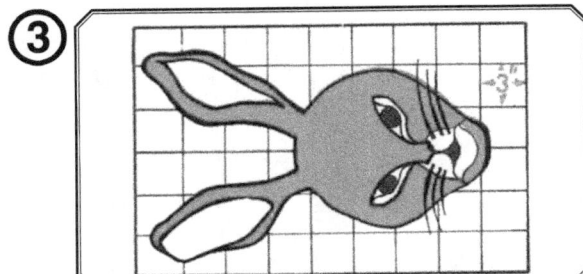
Draw and cut pattern for the face from card 27" X 18". Cut holes for eyes. Use paints or coloured paper to decorate.

④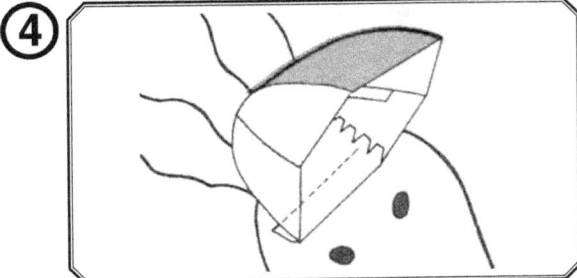
Glue cap to face, be sure you can see through eye holes. Cut and decorate sack or paper for body. Add tail.

Witch

①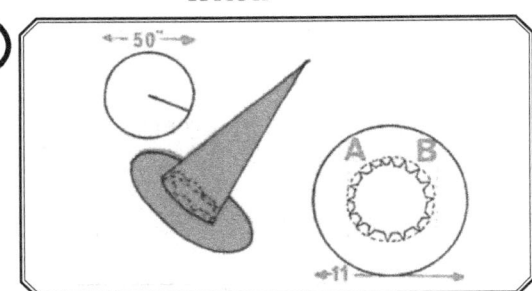
Make rim 11" in diameter. Cut hole with tab AB to fit your head. Make cone and glue to tabs on rim.

②
Draw and cut pattern for cat from thick card. Tape loop of string at back to carry it.

③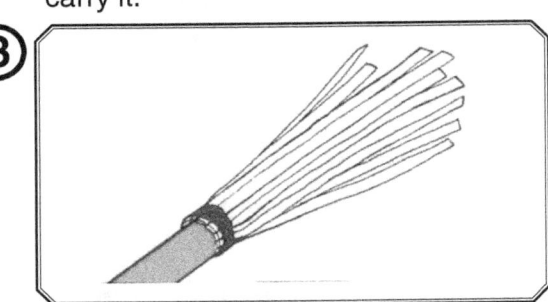
Tape the strips of brown paper to the piece of wood at one end to make a broom.

④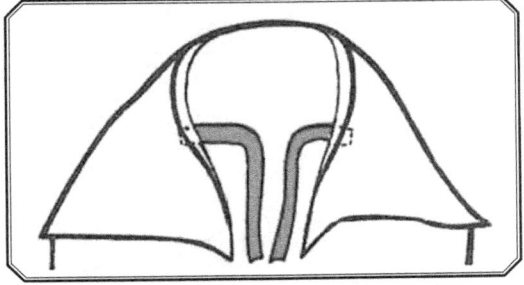
Cut 3 ft. of crepe paper and attach two cloth tapes to make cape.

29

Bedroom Furniture (Part 6)

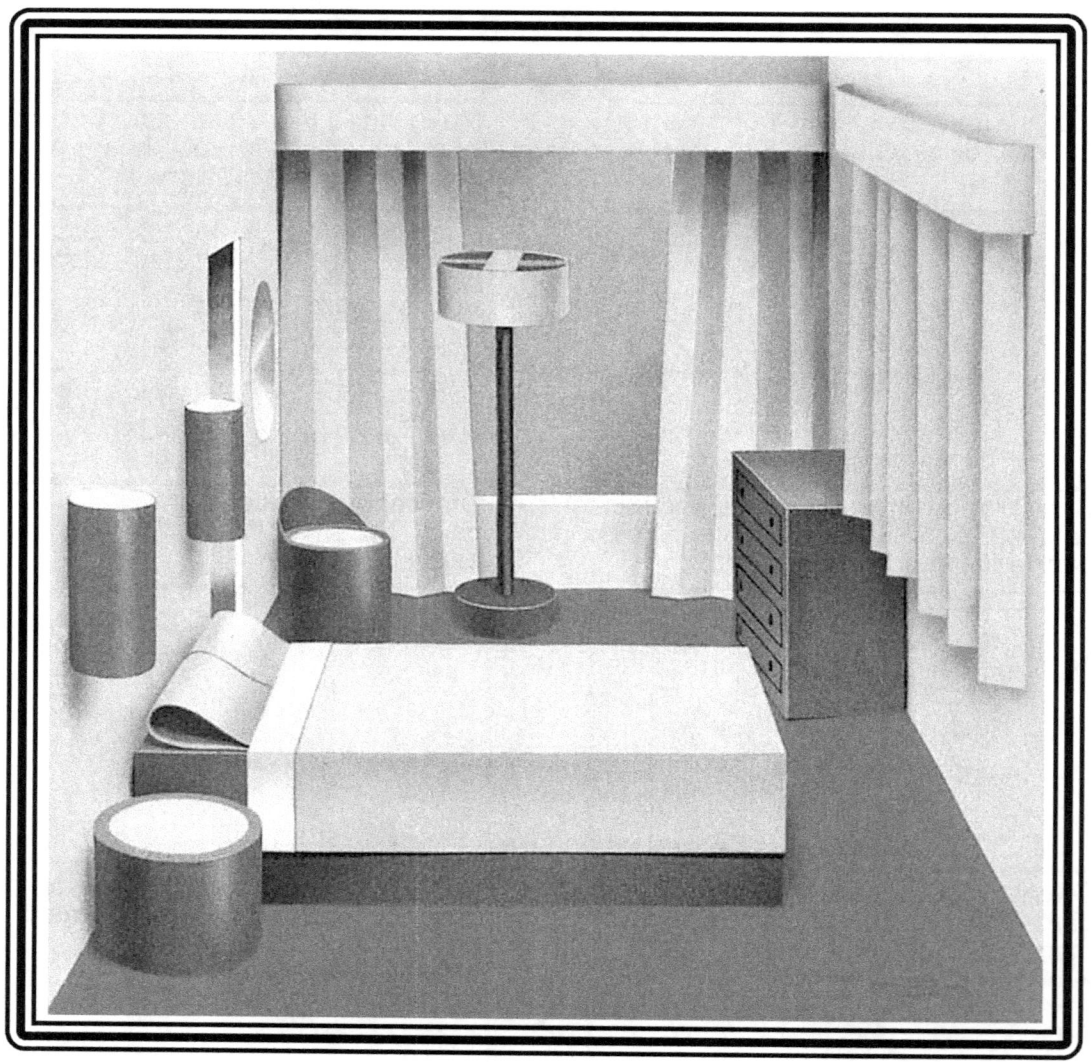

Materials Required

* Stiff coloured paper
* Lolly stick
* Thin coloured card
* Pencil, scissors, ruler glue, coloured paints

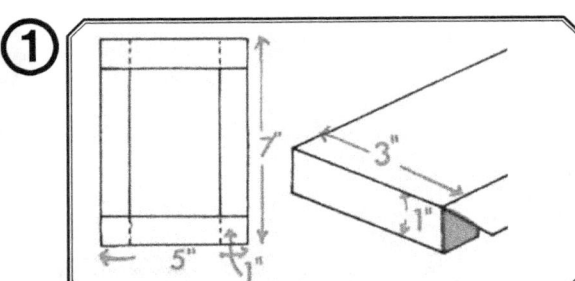

Draw and cut pattern for bed from card 7" X 5". Fold along lines and glue.

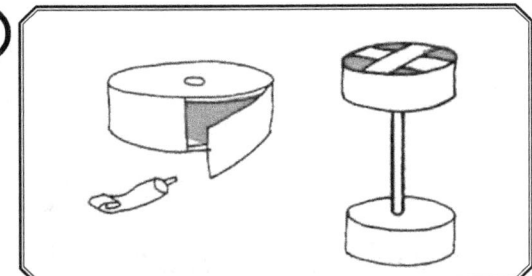

Make lamp base from two cardboard discs 1½" diameter and paper strip, as shown. Push stick in base and glue shade on top.

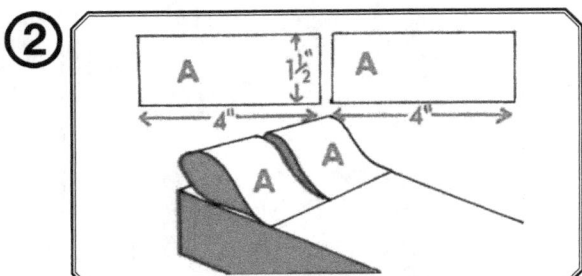

Fold 2 pieces of thin card 4" X 1½" as shown. Glue to top of bed for pillows.

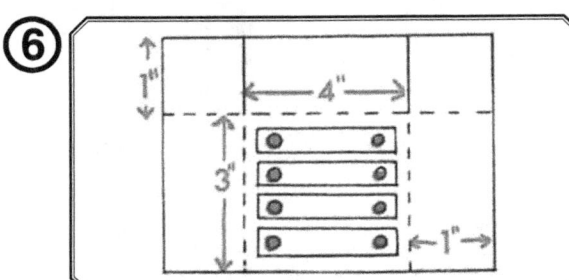

Draw and cut card 6" X 4" for chest of drawers. Fold along dotted lines and glue. Decorate with paints.

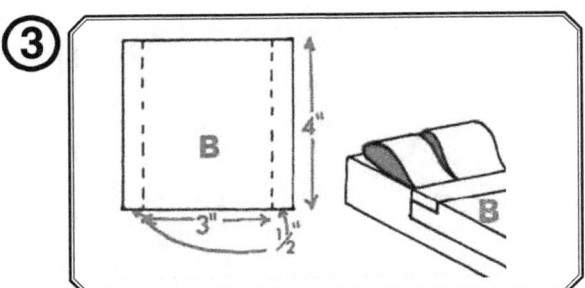

Fold piece of paper 4" X 4" as shown, and glue on bed for bedspread. Add strip of white paper for sheet.

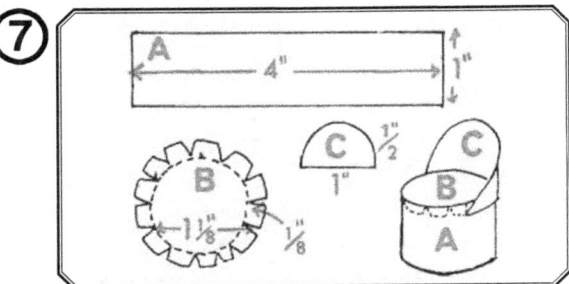

Draw and cut patterns for two seats from card. Roll 4" strips into tubes and glue on cushions and packs.

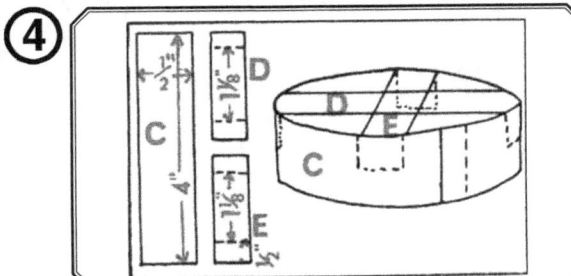

Draw and cut paper patterns for lampshade and glue together as shown.

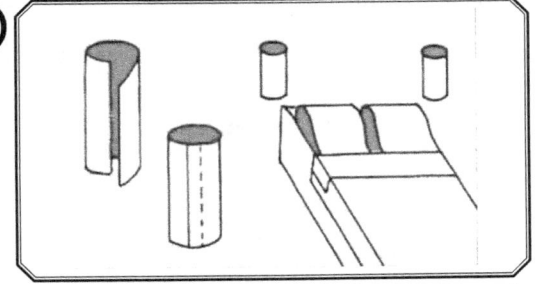

Make wall-lights from 1" squares of paper. Roll into tubes and glue to wall above bed.

30

Spinner

Materials Required

- Two cotton reels
- 2 ft. of thin string
- Two cardboard discs 3" diameter
- Pencil
- Glue
- Good penknife, coloured paints

①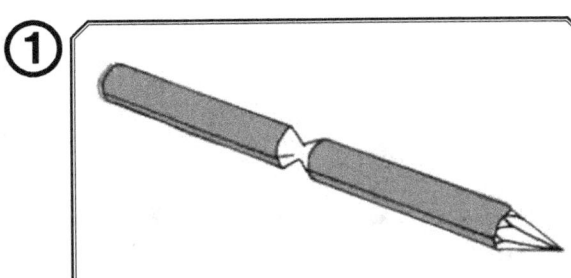
Notch the pencil in the middle as shown.

②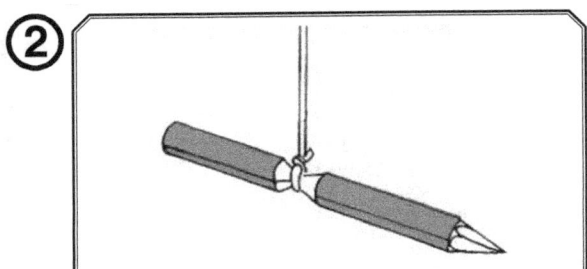
Place string in the notch and tie tightly.

③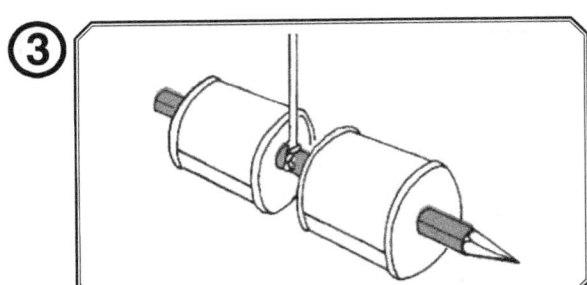
Fit two cotton reels tightly on the pencil with a gap of 1/8" left between them at the centre.

④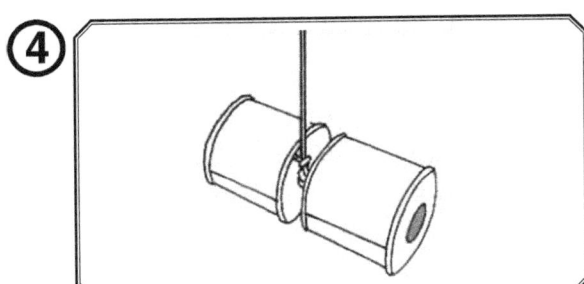
Cut off the overlapping pencil ends with a good penknife.

⑤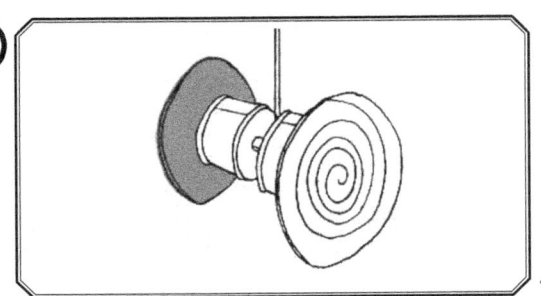
Paint designs on cardboard discs and glue them on outside edges of reels.

⑥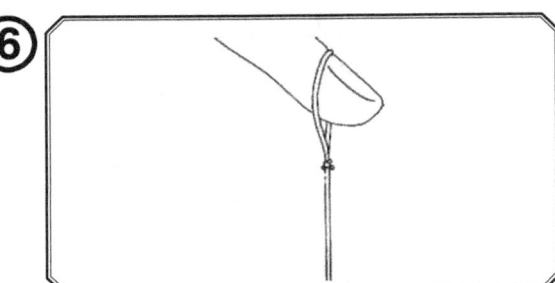
Tie a loop in the end of the string to fit your finger through.

⑦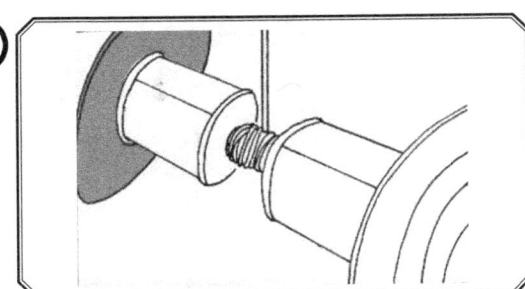
Wind string around pencil and allow your spinner to fall.

⑧
Jerk it upwards when it's at the end of the string to keep it spinning.

Cotton Reel Caterpillar and Bottle Top Mobile (Wind Chime)

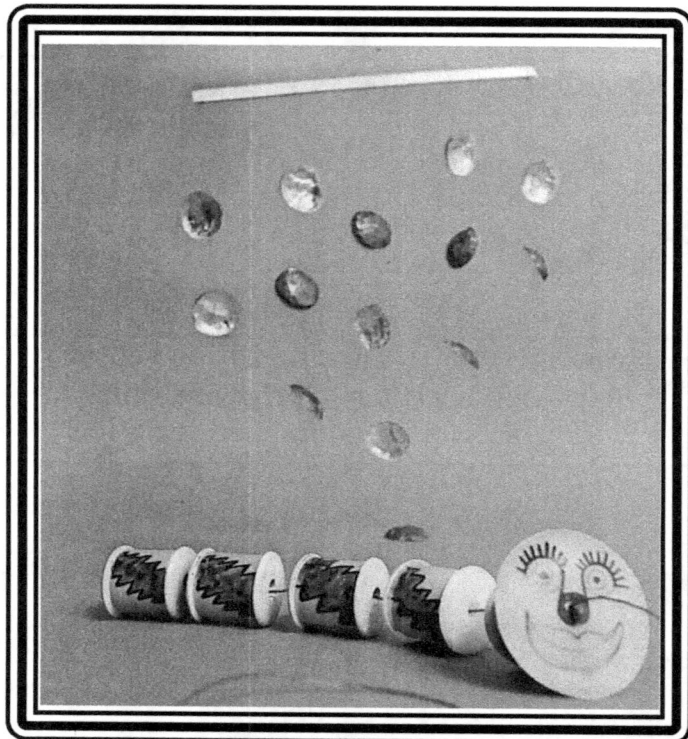

Materials Required

Cotton Real Caterpillar
* Five Cotton reels
* Thick card disc 2½" diameter
* Thick card disc 1" diameter
* Piece white paper 5" square to cover reels
* 9" length of elastic
* Two small buttons
* Thin string (approx 1 yard)
* Glue, pencil, good penknife
* Coloured paints

Bottle Top Mobile
* Fourteen metal foil Bottles tops
* Piece thick card ½" x 12"
* 5' length black cotton
* 2' length black cotton

Cotton Real Caterpillar

①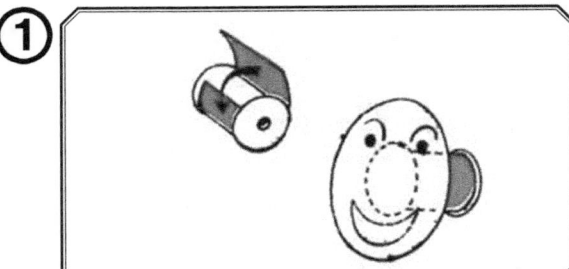
Cover reels with white paper. Paint face on large card disc and glue one reel to centre of other side.

②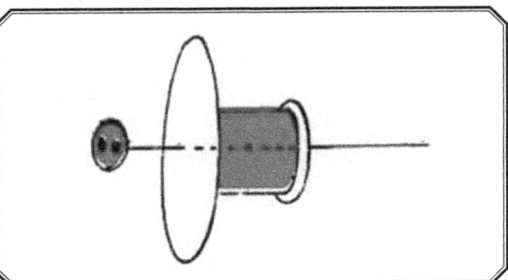
Pierce hole in centre of face. Tie elastic to one button and thread other end through hole.

③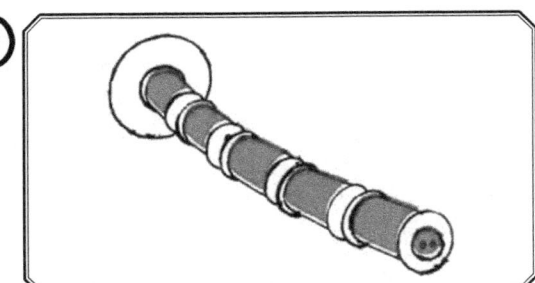
Thread on remaining reels. Tie end to other button. Decorate body reels.

④
Tie end of string to button on face. Pull your caterpillar along and watch him wriggle.

Bottle Top Mobile

①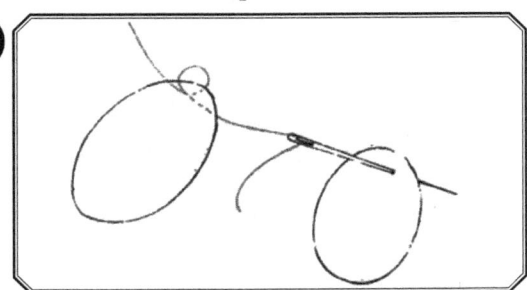
Smooth out creases in the bottle tops and using needle, thread each one with your needle onto 5 ft of cotton.

②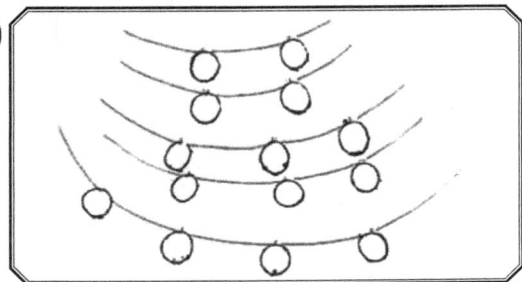
Space tops evenly along the cotton and cut two lengths 8", two lengths 10½" and one length 17".

③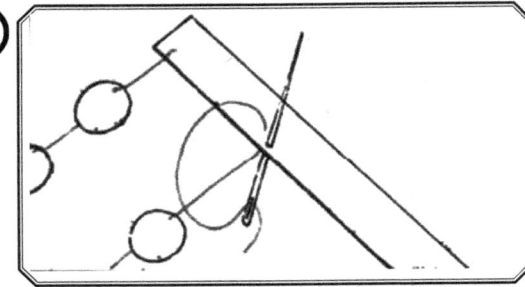
Sew one end of each strand onto the card.

④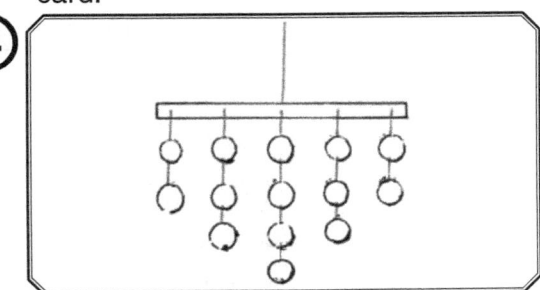
Secure the bottle tops by knotting the free ends. Then trim off any excess. Sew a 2 ft length of cotton to the middle of the card and hang your mobile up.

32

Pin Cushion and Paper Earrings

Materials Required

Pin Cushion
* Two discs of cloth 5" diameter
* Scraps of cloth for stuffing
* Scraps of coloured felt
* Two buttons for eyes
* 2" piece of cloth tape
* Scissors, needle and thread
* Wool

Paper Earrings
* Two discs of stiff coloured Paper 2" diameter
* Two strips of paper 2" × 1"
* Glue
* Pencil, scissors, needle and thread

Pin Cushion

①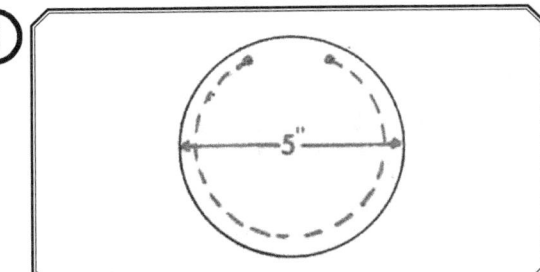

Sew cloth discs together with the best side inwards. Leave space at top. Turn inside out.

②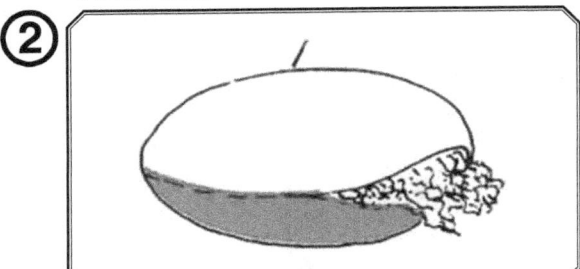

Stuff with scraps of cloth. Then sew together at top.

③

Sew tapes onto cushion to make a loop. Sew on piece of coloured felt, and buttons for eyes and mouth. Add wool for hair.

④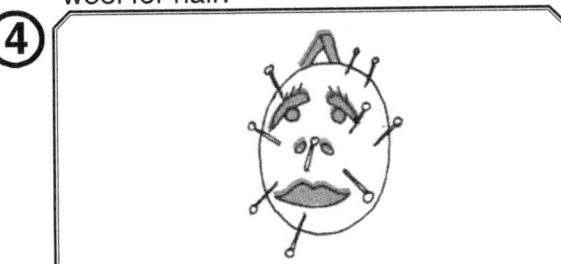

Now your cushion is ready to be stuck full of pins and needles!

Paper Earrings

①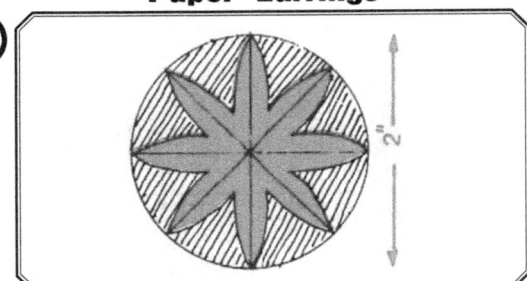

Draw and cut out pattern as shown from discs of coloured paper. Curl up ends of petals.

②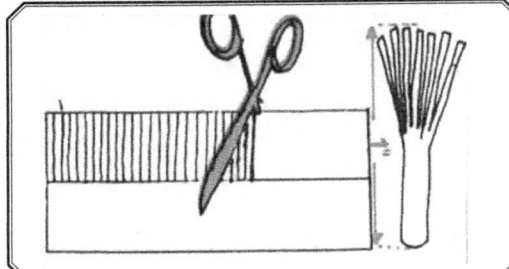

Make ½" cuts right along 2" strips of paper. Roll the strips and glue edges. Push strands outwards.

③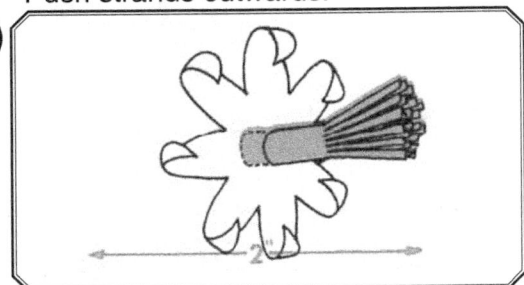

Make a hole in the centre of each flower large enough to fit the rolled.

④

Push strips through centres of flowers. Push needle and thread through back and tie as shown to make loops to fit over ears.

Fairy and Queen Costumes

Materials Required

Fairy
* White crepe paper 24" × 20"
* Thin card 24" × 3"
* Four pieces of thin card 3" Square
* Thin card 28" × 20"
* Very thick card 14" × 14"
* 30" length of cloth tape
* Tin foil
* String
* Glue and Cellotape
* Scissors, pencil

Queen
* Stiff card
* Crepe paper
* Cotton wool
* Black paper
* Tin foil
* Two 12" long pieces of Cloth tape
* Small piece of coloured Paper
* 36" of string
* Glue and Cellotape
* Scissors, pencil, ruler

Fairy

①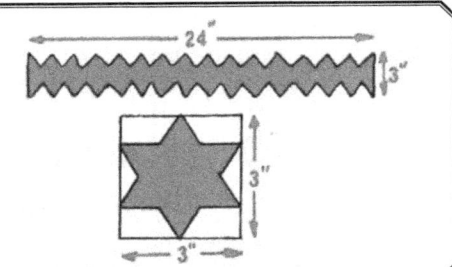

Draw and cut the above pattern for the crown from foil covered card 24" X 3". Cut pattern for four stars from pieces of card 3" square.

②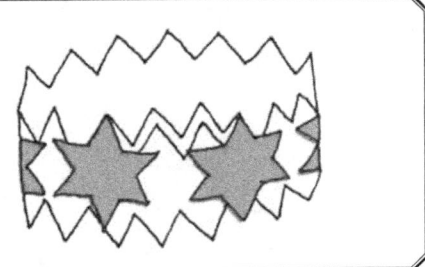

Glue the stars to the band to make a crown. Tape the band so that it will fit your head.

③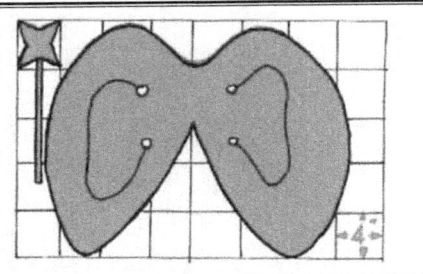

Draw and cut wand from foil covered card 14" X 4". Draw and cut wings from foil covered card 28" X 20". Pierce holes and attach string to fit wings.

④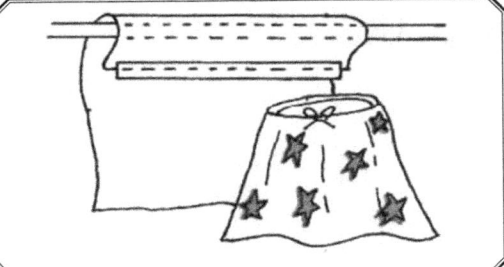

Lay cloth tape along 24" edge of crepe paper, fold and tape. Decorate with foil stars. Tie around your waist for skirt.

Queen

①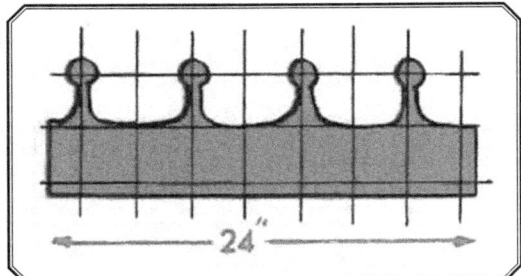

Cut and draw pattern as shown from the stiff card to fit your head.

②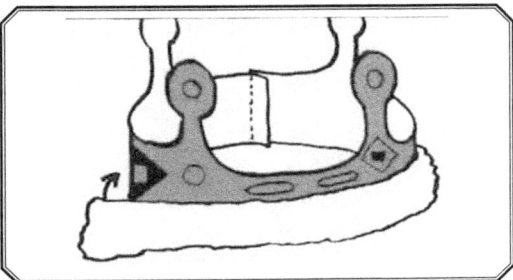

Glue ends together to form crown. Decorate with foil and coloured paper as shown and add cotton wool to the base.

③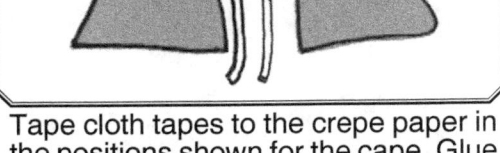

Tape cloth tapes to the crepe paper in the positions shown for the cape. Glue cotton wool around collar for trim.

④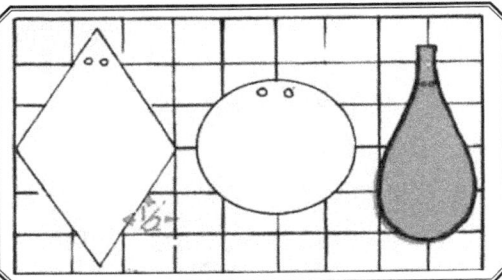

Glue black paper dots to cotton wool. Cut shapes from card, decorate and string together to make royal necklace.

34

Hall and Landing Furniture (Part 7)

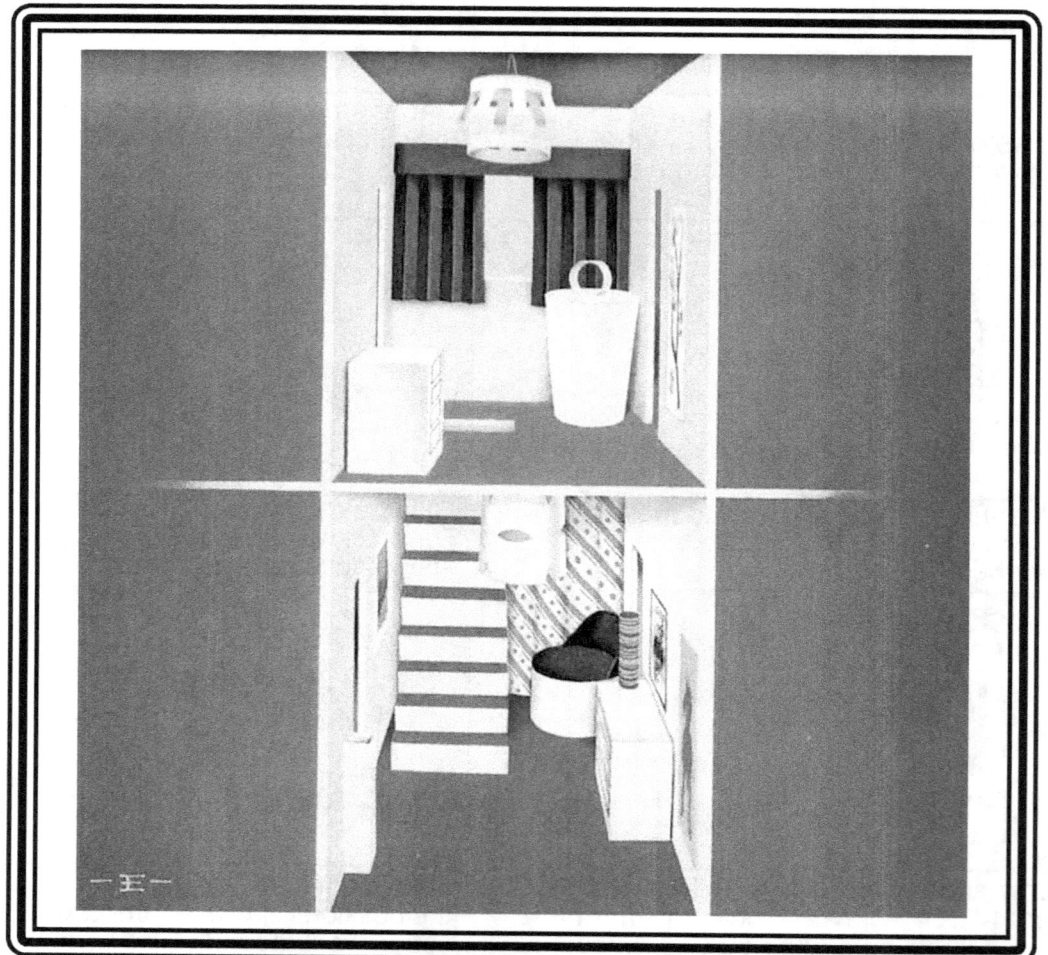

Materials Required

* Coloured paper
* Thin card
* Coloured paints
* Scissors, glue, pencil, ruler

①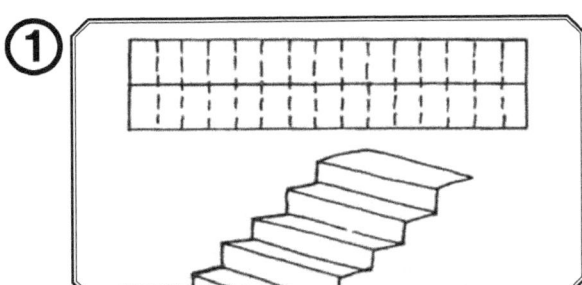
Make the stairs from card 10½" × 2". Fold on dotted lines as shown.

⑤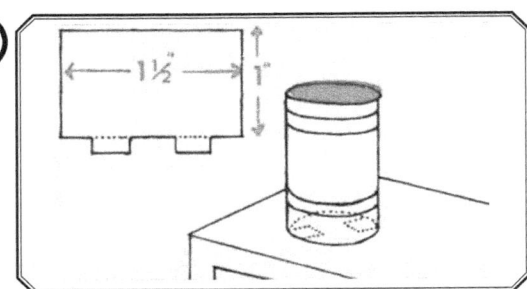
Draw and cut pattern for lamp on a 1¼" × 1½" piece of paper. Roll and glue as shown. Glue onto hall chest.

②
Glue one end of the staircase to hall floor and the other end to the opening in the landing floor.

⑥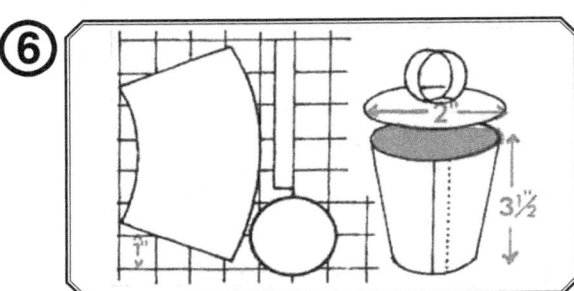
Draw and cut pattern for basket from card 8" × 7". Bend and glue. Glue on 2" diameter disc for lid. Add paper handle.

③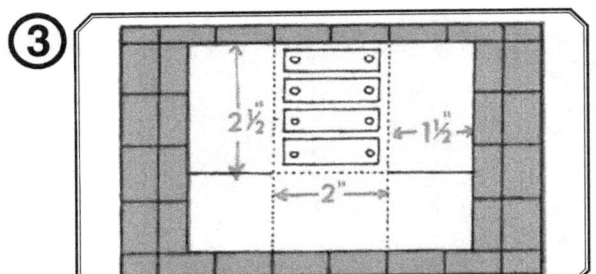
Draw and cut pattern for landing chest from card. Fold along dotted lines and glue together. Decorate.

⑦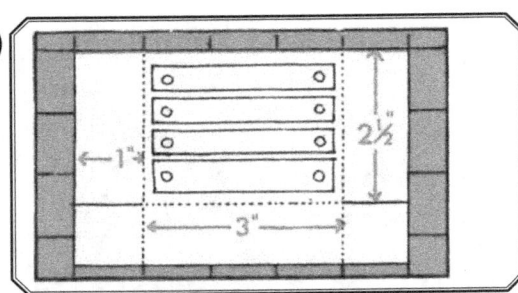
Draw and cut pattern for hall chest from card. Fold along dotted lines and glue together. Decorate as shown.

④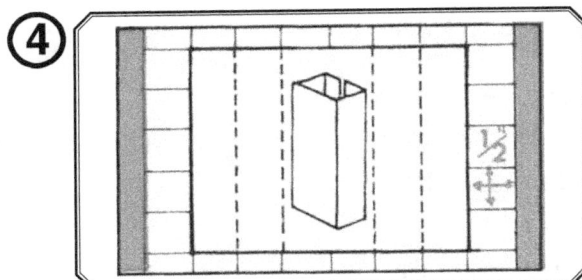
Draw and cut pattern for umbrella stand from card 3" × 2½". Fold on dotted lines and glue to wall in hall.

⑧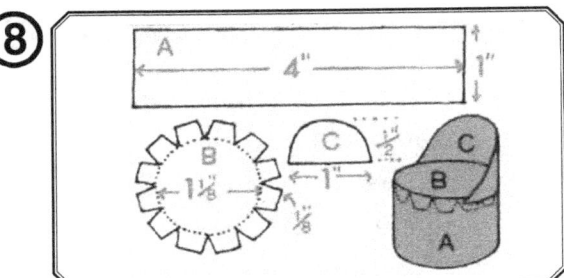
Draw and cut pattern for hall chair from card. Roll 4" strip into tube and glue on cushion and back.

35
Cork Models

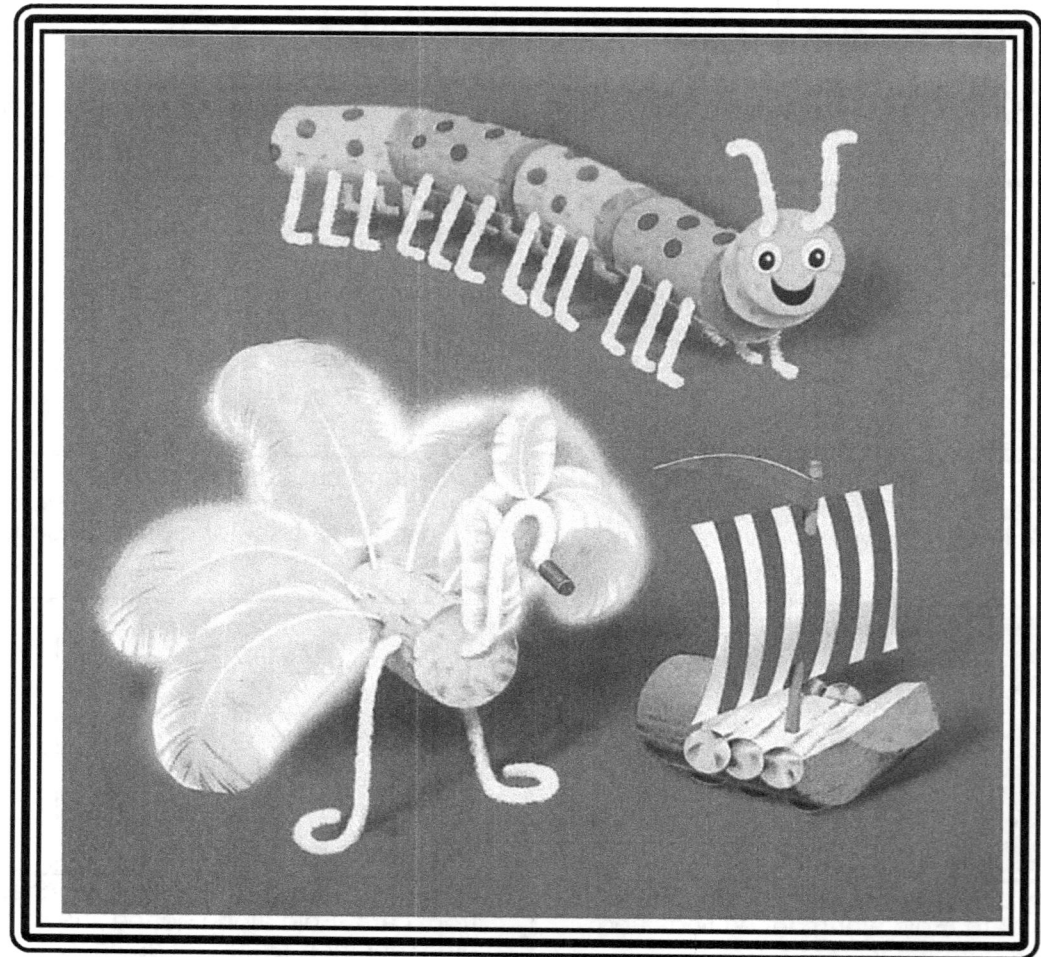

Materials Required

- Six ¼" diameter foil discs
- Seven corks
- Feathers
- Pipe cleaners
- Cocktail stick
- Drawing pins
- Small nail
- Penknife
- ¼" length of coloured drinking straw
- Glue, scissors
- Paper
- Coloured paints

Make holes in cork with nail. Push in feathers as shown and two pieces of pipe cleaner to make legs.

 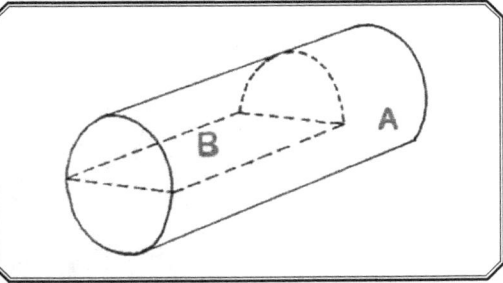

To make a galleon cut a cork into two pieces, as shown. Be careful when you are cutting.

Push a pipe cleaner into the front of cork for neck. Glue on head feathers and add pieces of straw for beak.

 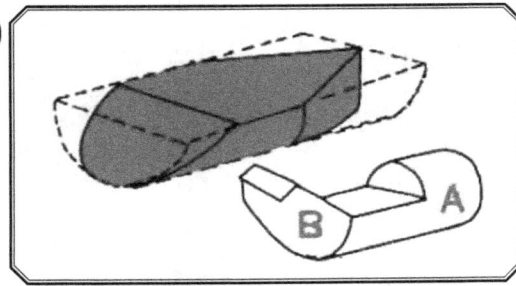

Shape piece B with scissors for prow of ship. Glue it to the front of piece A.

 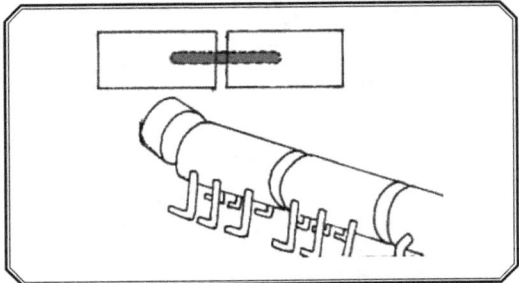

For centipede, join 4½" corks together with pipe cleaners. Push six pieces of pipe cleaner into each body cork for legs.

 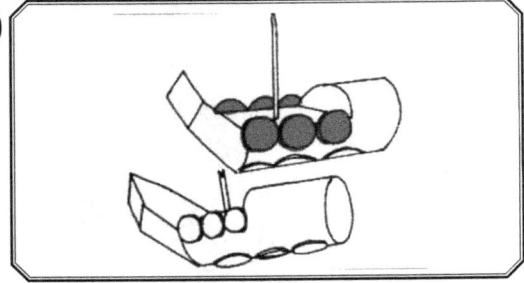

Add drawing pins to bottom to add weight to the keel. Glue foil discs to sides for shields.

 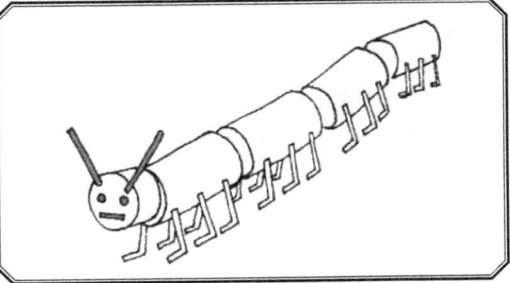

Push two pieces of pipe cleaner into head section for horns. Paint and decorate your centipede.

 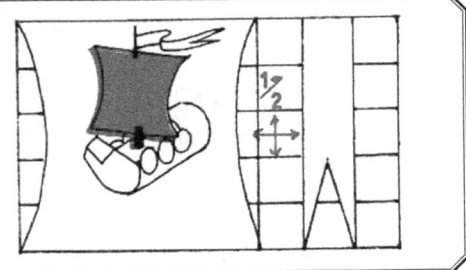

Cut patterns from paper for sail and flag. Push cocktail stick into hull then fix them into position. Watch it float.

36

Party Place Names and Party Sweet Tree

Materials Required

Party Place Names
* Piece of thick paper 5" × 7" for each guest
* Ruler, coloured paints
* Scissors, pencil

Party Sweet Tree
* One paper or plastic cup full of earth
* Small branch
* Cotton
* Wrapped sweets
* Coloured paints or silver foil

Party Place Names

①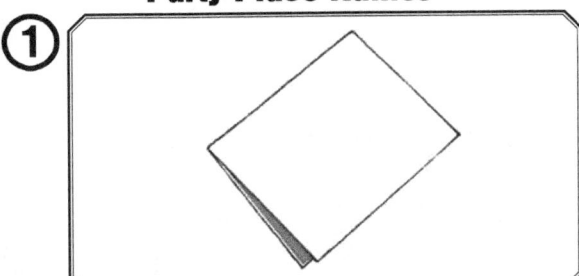
Fold paper in half.

②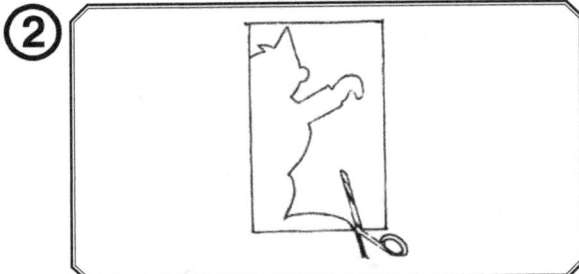
Draw the outline of your clown with his back to the fold. Cut round the shape but do not cut along the fold.

③
Paint both sides of your clown and write the name of one of your guests on his shirt.

④
Make a different coloured clown for each guest. Hang the clowns onto the sides of your guests' glasses.

Party Sweet Tree

①
Decorate cup with paints or cover with silver foil. Fill with earth.

②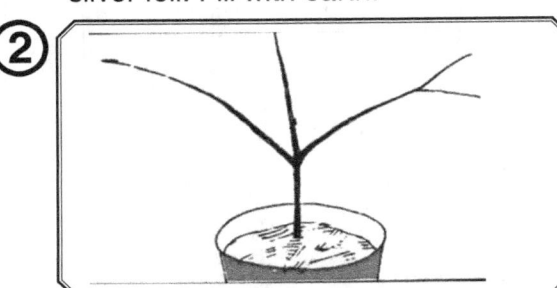
Push the small branch firmly into the earth.

③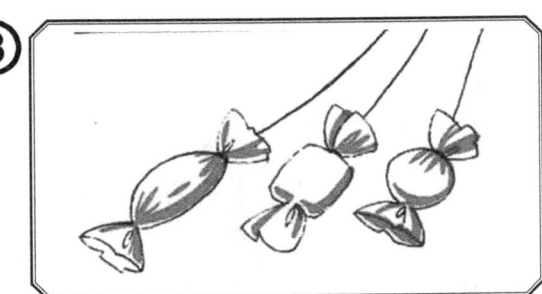
Tie short length of cotton to the end each sweet.

④
Hang the sweets on the "tree". Make sure there are enough sweets for all your friends.

Soft Toy and Melon-Seed Necklace

Materials Required

Soft Toy
* Two discs of felt 10" diameter
* Scraps of different coloured felt
* Scraps of cloth for stuffing
* Coloured wool
* Scissors, needle and thread

Melon-Seed Necklace
* Dozens of dried melon seeds
* Strong thread 24" long
* Needle

Soft Toy

①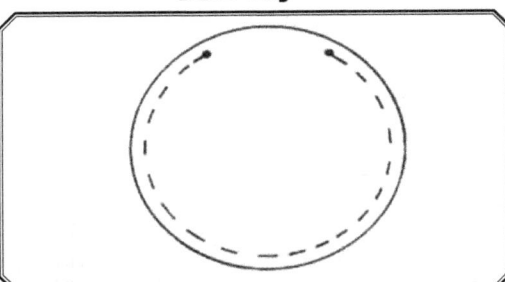
Sew 2 felt circles together, leaving 6" gap to put in stuffing. Turn inside out to hide stitching.

②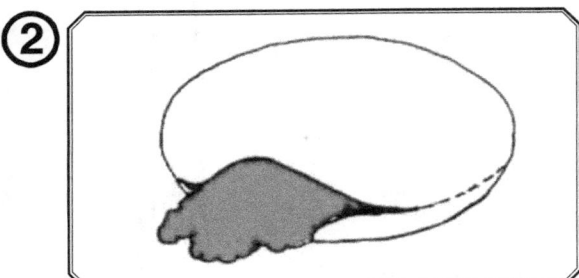
Stuff the body with scraps of cloth, and finish sewing the circles together.

③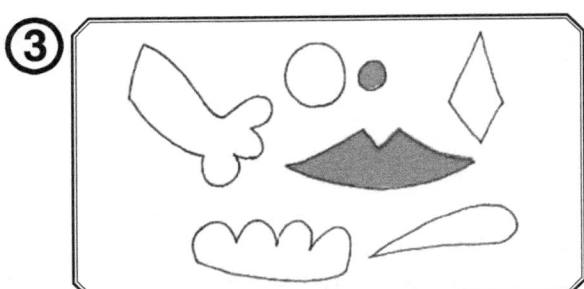
Cut out patterns from coloured felt for face, arms and feet. Sew them onto body.

④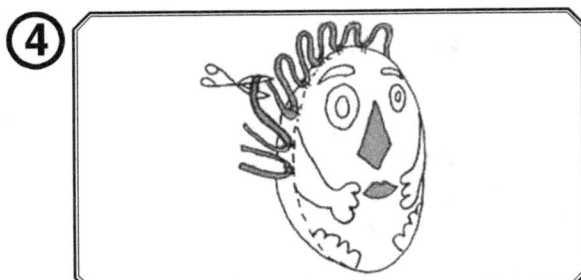
Sew on loops of coloured wool and cut ends to make hair.

Melon-Seed Necklace

①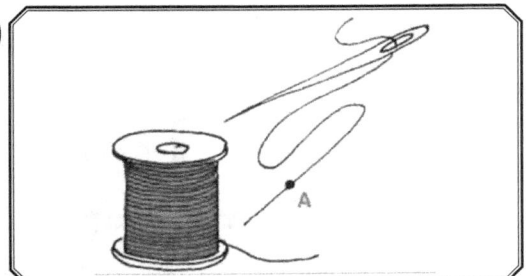
Knot one end of thread at A, 2" from end. Put other end of thread through needle.

②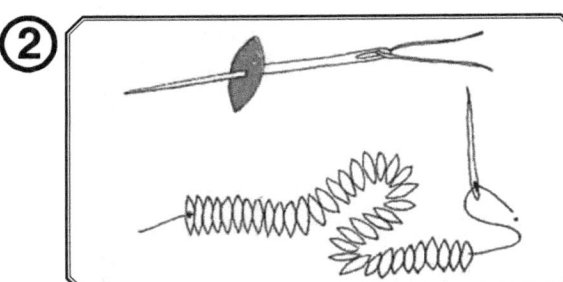
Push needle through middle of seed. Add more seeds until only 2" of thread is left.

③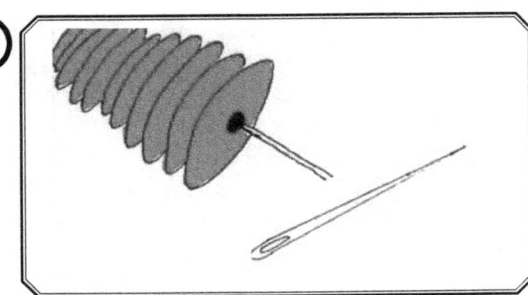
Take the needle off the thread, and knot the end as close as possible to the last seed.

④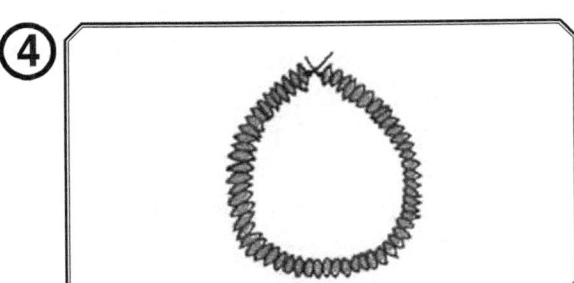
Tie 2 ends together to complete your necklace.

38

Lion Costume

Materials Required

- Thin card 22" × 5"
- Thin card 20" × 24"
- Two discs of thin card 10" diameter
- Small pieces of coloured paper for decoration
- Paper sack or large sheet of brown paper
- Stiff paper for tail
- Glue and Cellotape
- Scissors, pencil and
- coloured paints

①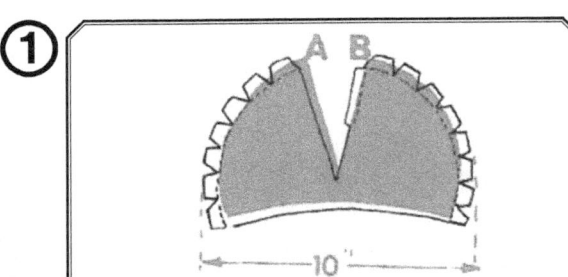
Cut the pattern shown from the two 10" card discs. Glue tab B to point A.

②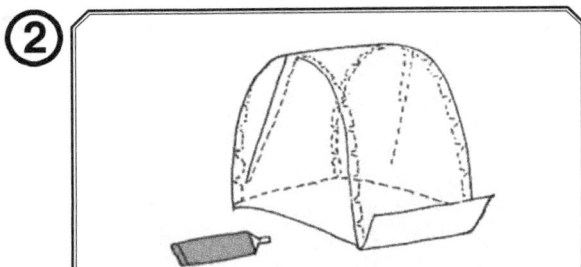
Bend disc tabs inwards and glue to thin card 22" X 5" to form the cap. Fold back a flap at top edge of cap.

③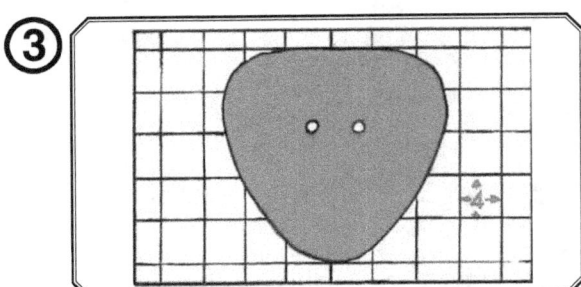
Draw and cut pattern for the face from card 20" X 24". Cut holes for eyes.

④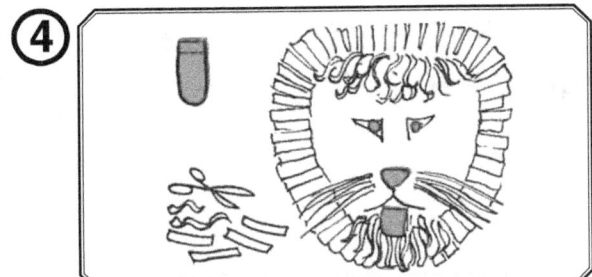
Decorate the lion's face by adding strips of paper for his whiskers, mane, tongue and nose.

⑤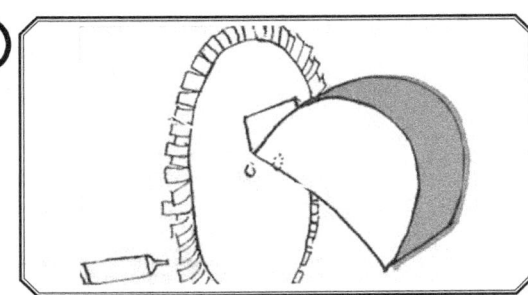
Glue cap to face but be sure you can see through eye holes.

⑥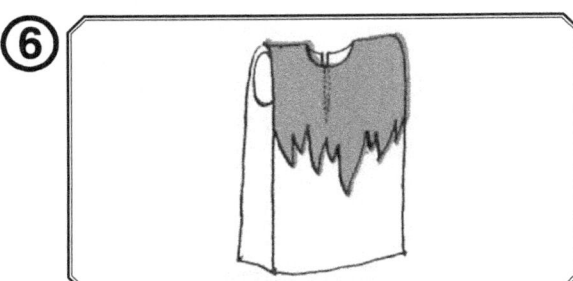
Cut pattern for body from paper sack or from folded sheet of brown paper. If using paper, tape sides. Decorate.

⑦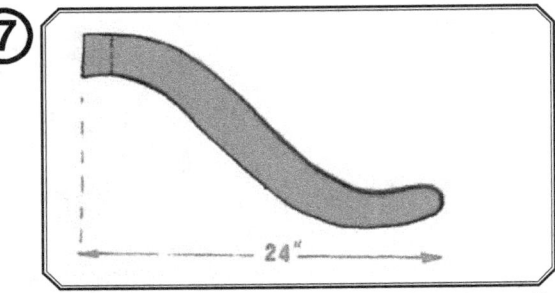
Draw and cut the pattern for the tail from paper. Glue it with tab to body sack as shown.

⑧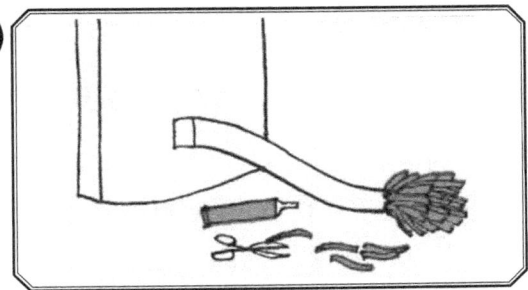
Cut tufts of wool and glue them to the end of the lion's tail to complete your lion.

39

Kitchen Furniture (Part 8)

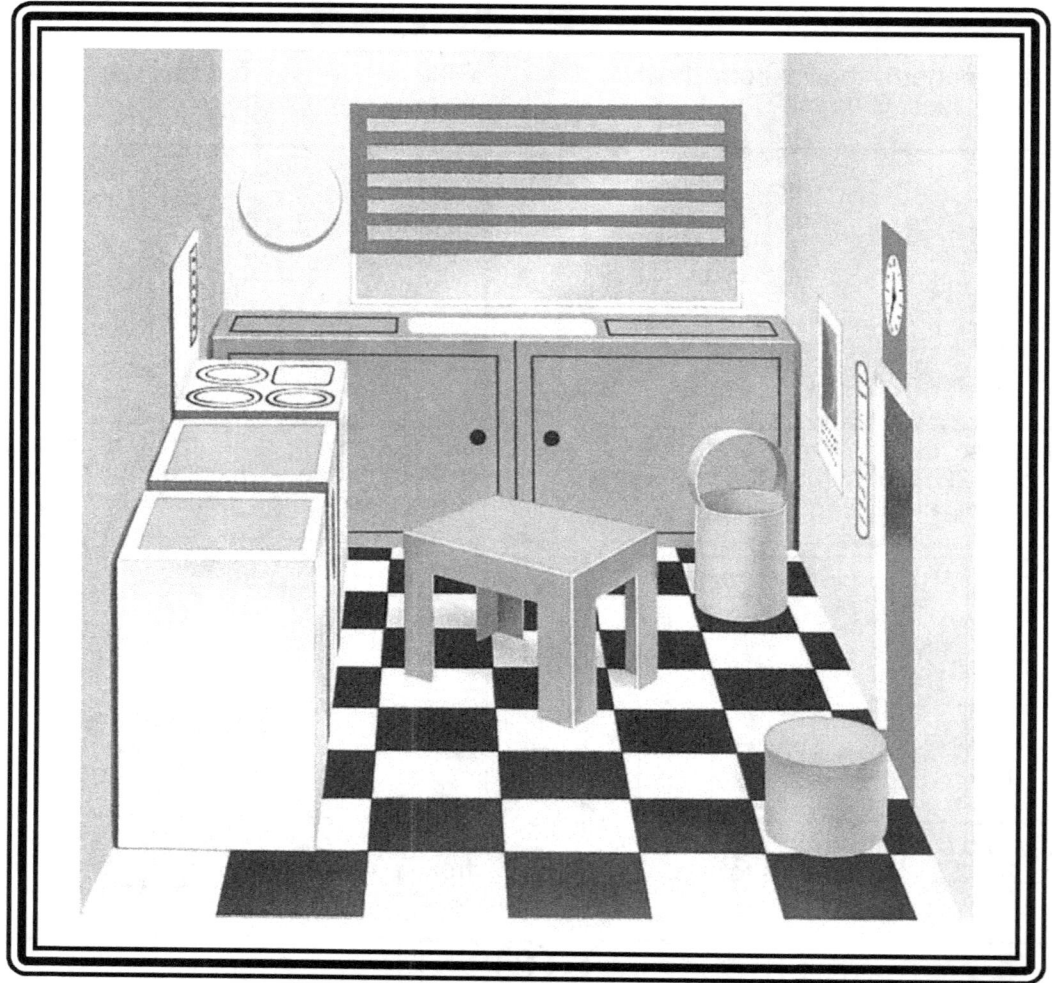

Materials Required

* Thin card
* Scissors, pencil, ruler
* Glue, coloured paints

①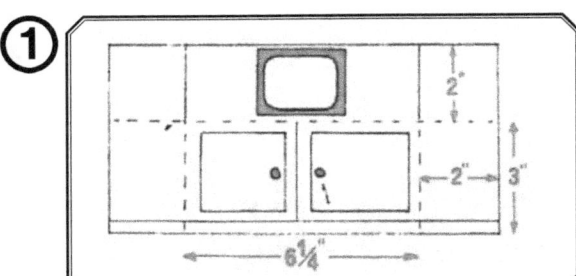
Draw and cut pattern above for sink unit from card. Fold along dotted lines.

②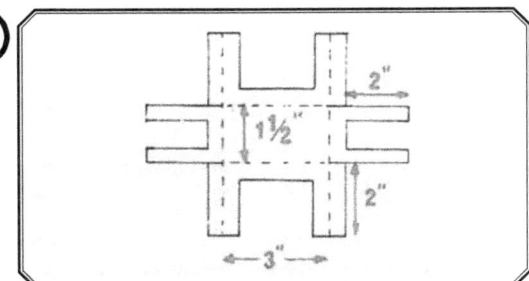
Glue together as shown, and decorate with paints. Place in position in kitchen

③
Draw and cut pattern above for washing machine from card. Fold along dotted and glue together. Decorate as shown.

④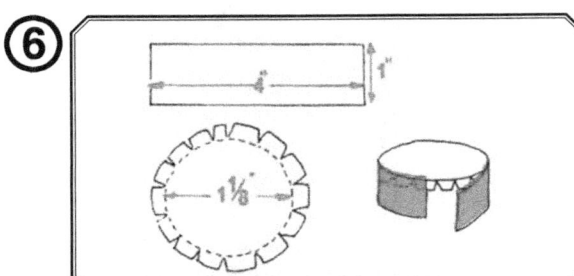
Draw and cut pattern for cooker from card. Fold along dotted lines and glue together. Decorate as shown

⑤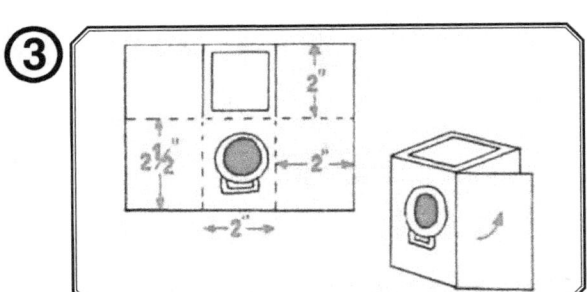
Draw pattern for table on card. Cut along solid lines, fold along dotted lines and glues.

⑥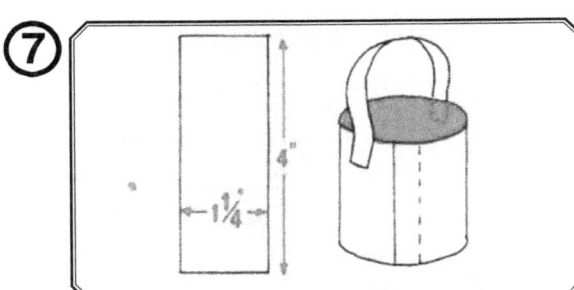
Draw and cut pattern for chair from card. Roll 4" strip into tube and glue on cushion as shown

⑦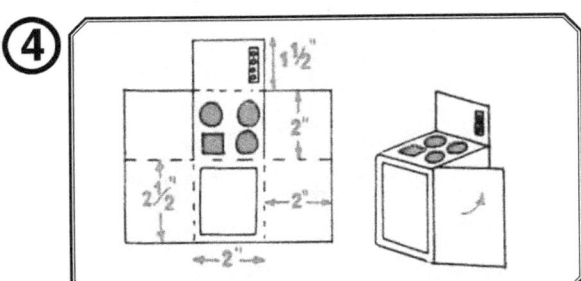
Draw and cut pattern for bucket from card. Roll 4" strip into tube and glue. Add small card strip for handle.

⑧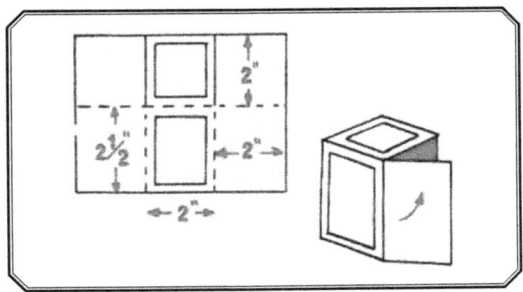
Draw and cut pattern for fridge from card. Fold along dotted lines and glue as shown. Decorate with paints.

40

Doll's Shop and Nurse's Outfit

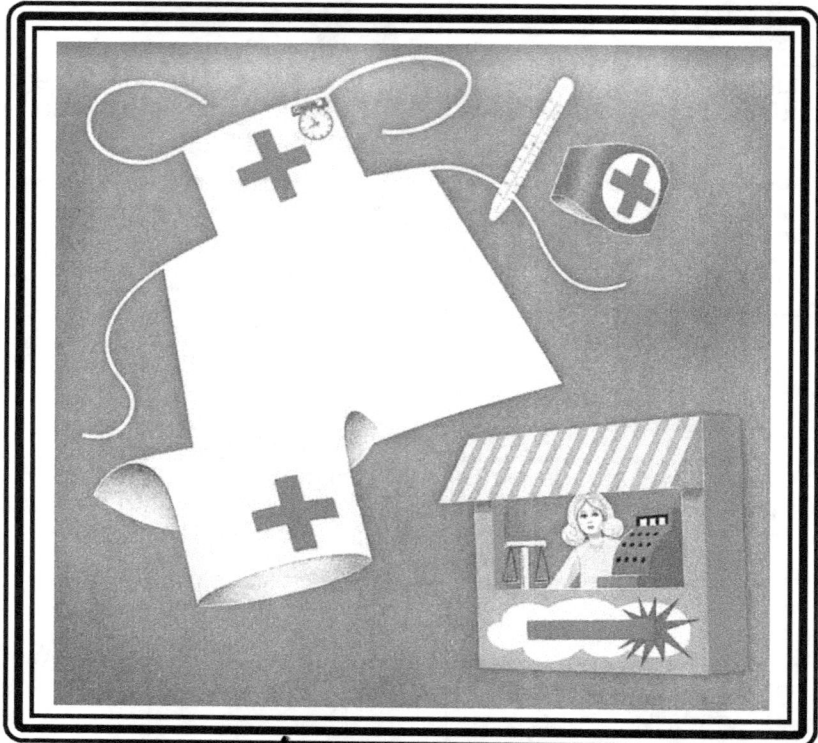

Material Required

Doll's Shop
* Sheet of thin card 12" × 15" (A)
* Strip of thin card 13" × 2"
* Piece of thin card 4½" × 3"
* Dowel 1½" long × 1/8" dia.
* Drinking straw
* One pine
* Two discs of paper ½"
* diameter
* Disc of paper 1" diameter
* Glue
* Pencil, scissors, needle and thread, coloured paints

Nurse's Outfit
* Piece of thin card 13" × 25"
* Piece of thin white card, or White material 18" × 24"
* Four cloth tapes 36" long × ½" wide
* Piece of card for watch.
* Armband and thermometer
* Glue
* Pencil, scissors, coloured paints

Doll's Shop

①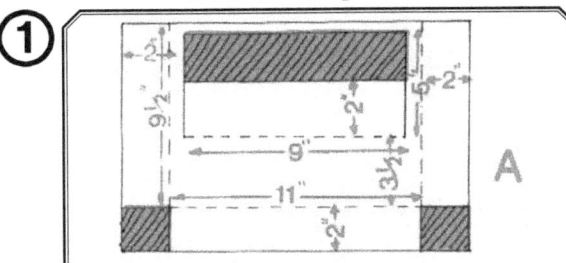

Draw and cut out pattern for shop front from card 12" X 15". Fold on dotted lines.

②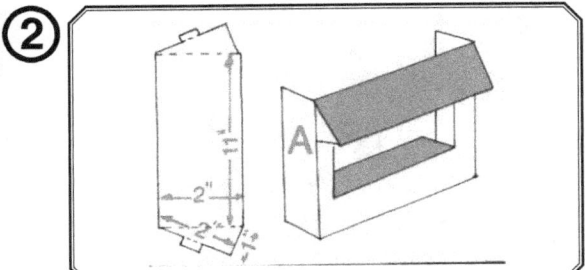

Cut out the roof from card 13" X 2". Fold and glue it onto shop front. Paint with bright colours.

③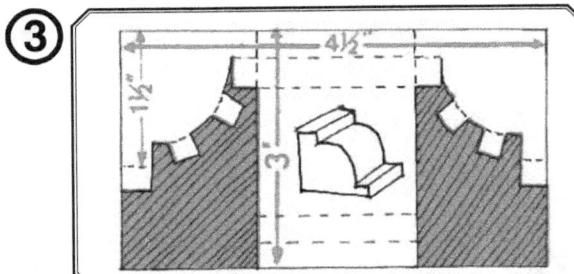

Cut pattern from piece of card 4 ½" X 3" to make cash register. Fold and glue tabs inside.

④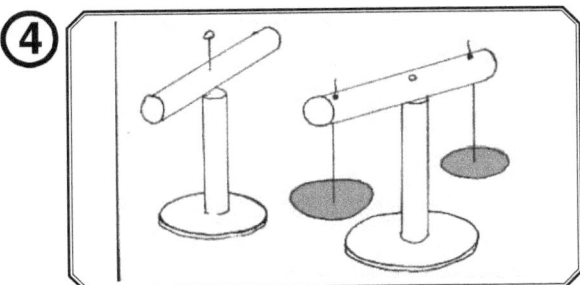

Pin straw to dowel. Thread ½" discs and glue dowel to 1" base disc to make shop scales.

Nurse's Outfit

①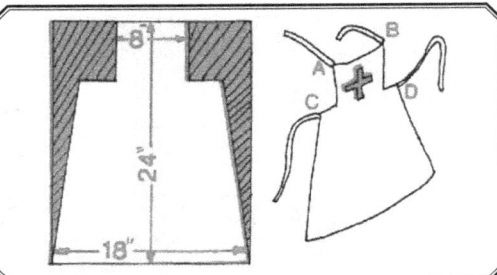

Draw and cut out pattern for apron. Glue on tapes as shown, at A, B, C and D.

②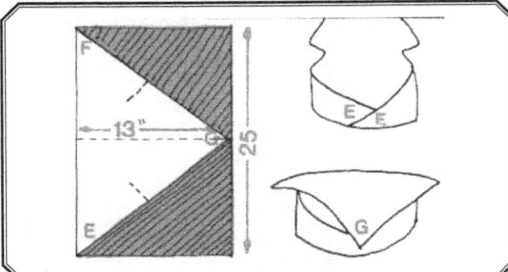

Cut pattern for cap. Cut along dotted lines, then glue E and F together. Bring G down to join them.

③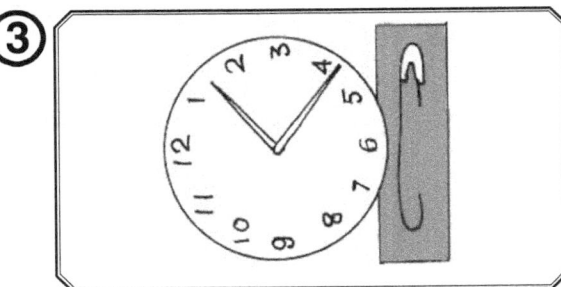

Draw and cut pattern for watch. Pin onto top of apron.

④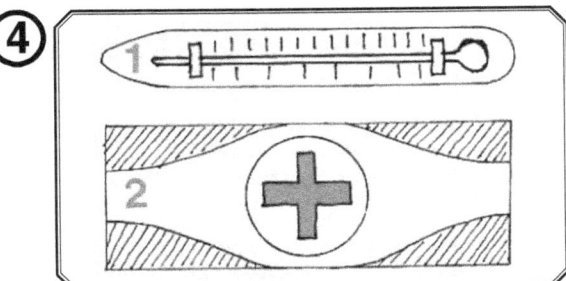

Draw and cut patterns for thermometer and armband. Then decorate as shown.

41
Rose

Materials Required

- Green and red crepe paper
- Glue
- Cellotape
- Thin wire
- Thin Card
- Scissors
- Sturdy wire (Flexible)

①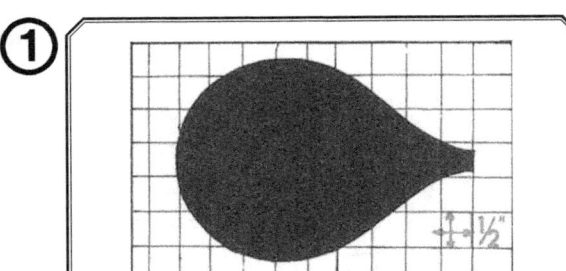
Draw and cut pattern above from card for petal shape.

②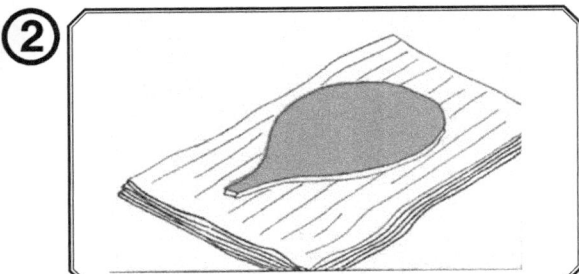
Fold crepe paper to eight thicknesses. Cut 16 petal shapes using card outline. Make sure grain of paper is vertical.

③
Stretch 4 of the crepe petals in the centre to form a hollow.

④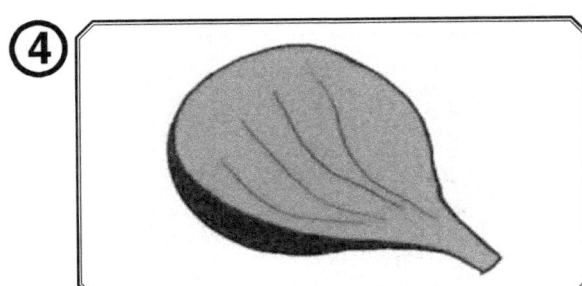
Stretch another 4 petals to make a slightly smaller hollow.

⑤
Take 4 more petals and make a very small hollow in these.

⑥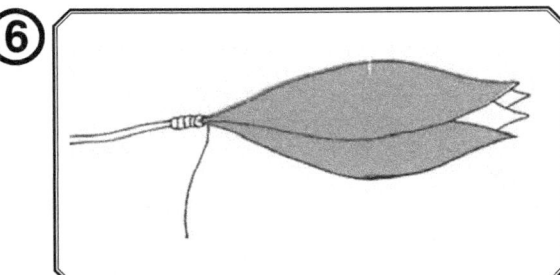
Take your last 4 petals and wrap at the top of your wire stem as shown. Attach at base with thin wire.

⑦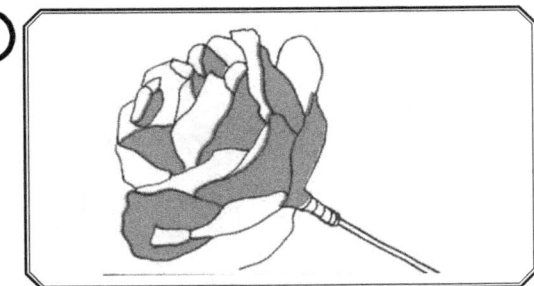
Add other petals, flattest first, until rose is complete. Secure with thin wire.

⑧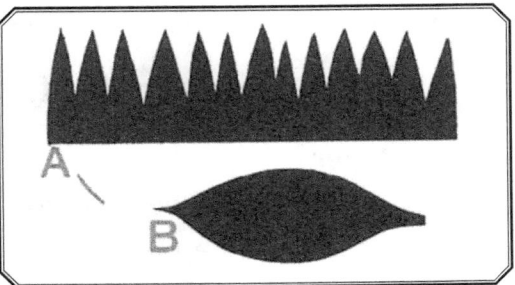
Draw and cut pattern shown from green crepe. Wrap A around bottom of rose and tape B onto stem for leaves. Paint stem green.

42

Book Cover and Construction Cards

Materials Required

Book Cover
- Large sheet of coloured paper
- Piece of white paper 3½" × 4"
- Old magazines
- Glue and Cellotape
- Pencil, scissors, ruler

Construction Cards
- Piece of thick card 9" × 12"
- Pencil and ruler
- Good penknife or scissors
- Coloured paints

Book Cover

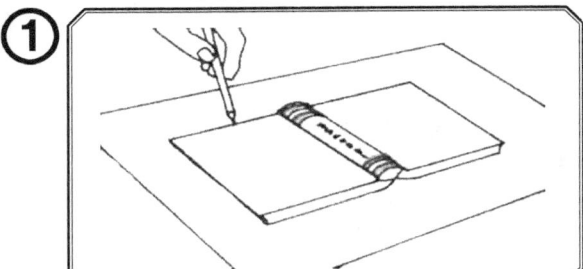

Open the book you wish to cover and place on coloured paper. Draw around it as shown.

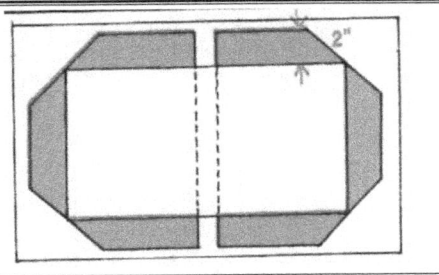

Add 2" tabs to edges of outline and cut finished pattern from sheet of paper.

Glue paper 3 ½" X 4" on front for title. Cut out magazine pictures and glue them to cover for decoration.

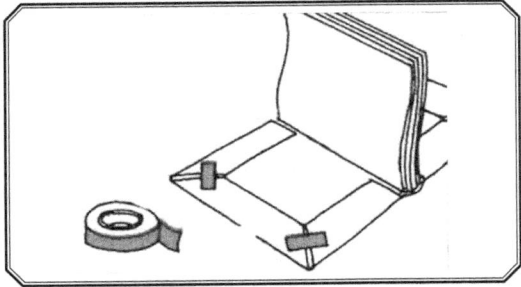

Turn cover and position book as shown. Fold tabs down and tape across corners.

Construction Cards

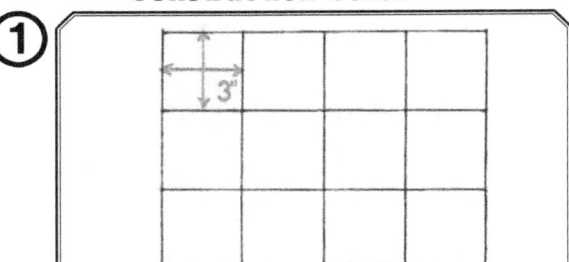

Draw and cut 12 squares from card 9" X 12"

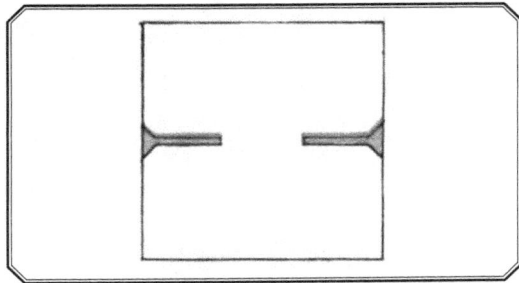

Cut 2 slots in each square at opposite edges 1" deep. Angle the corners of the slots.

Paint each card a different colour.

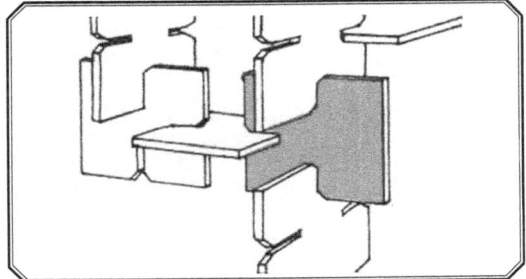

Now slot them together and see what you can build. Make more squares for bigger constructions.

43

Bathroom Furniture (Part 9)

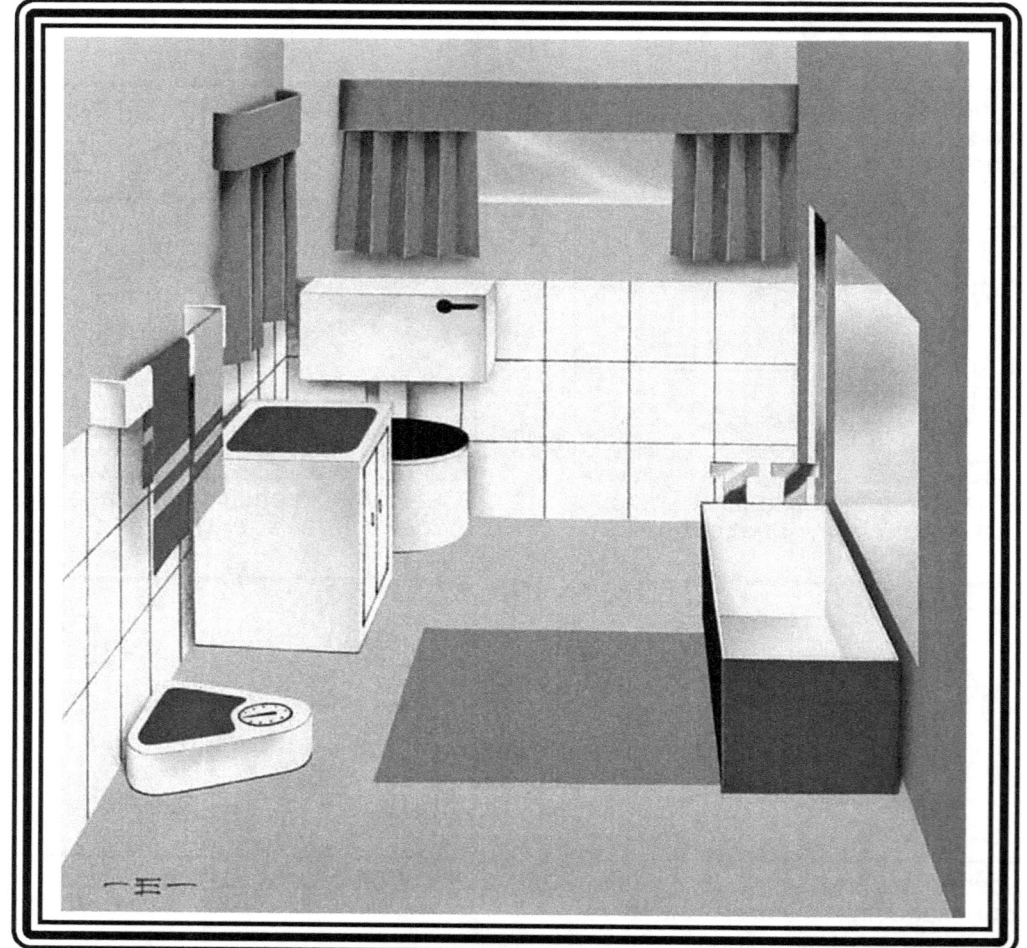

Materials Required

- Thick card ¼" × 3"
- Thin card
- Tin foil
- Toilet roll tube
- Coloured paper
- Scissors, glue, ruler, pencil
- Black paint

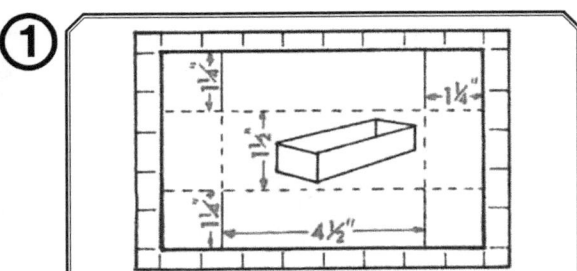

Draw pattern for bath on card 7" × 4". Cut along solid lines, fold along dotted lines and glue together

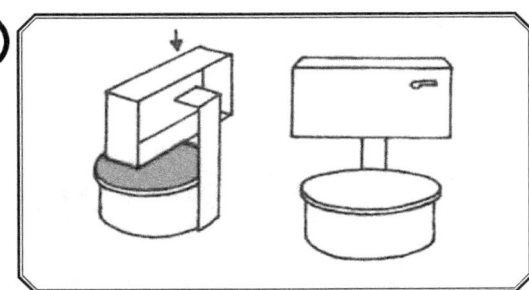

Fold ¼" of toilet upright over and glue on cistern as shown

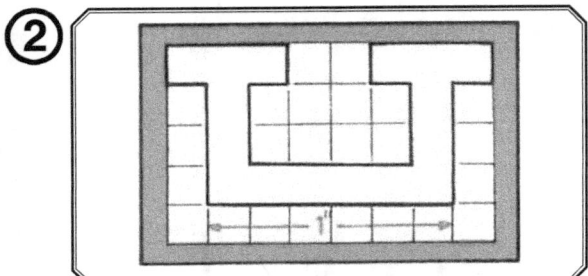

Glue foil onto card 1¼" × 1". Draw and cut pattern above for bath taps from it and glue into position

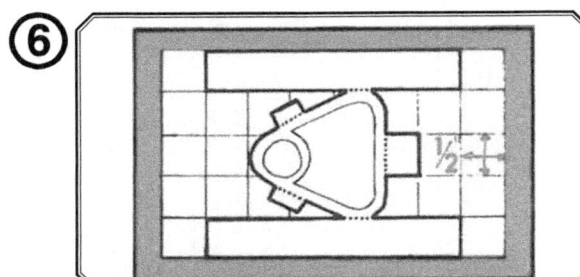

Draw and cut pattern for scales from card 3" ×2½". Fold along dotted lines and glue together. Decorate with paint

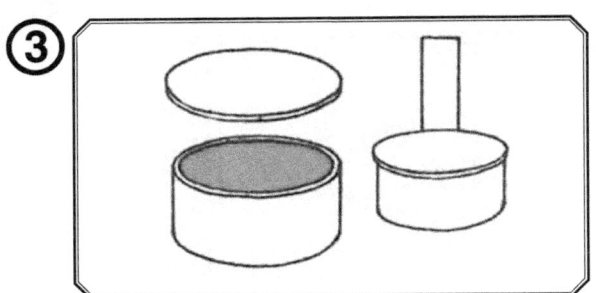

Cut a 1" piece of tube for toilet. Glue a paper disc on the top. Glue ¼" × 3" thick card in position shown

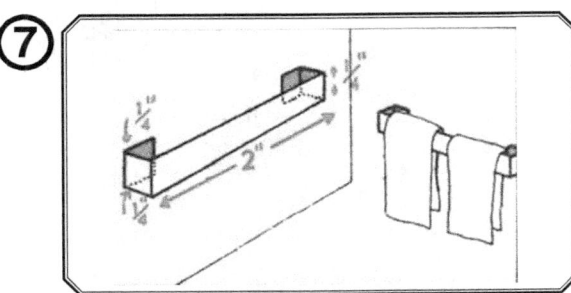

Cut and fold 3" × ¼" for towel rail. Glue to wall. Cut two pieces of paper 2" ׾", fold and hang as shown.

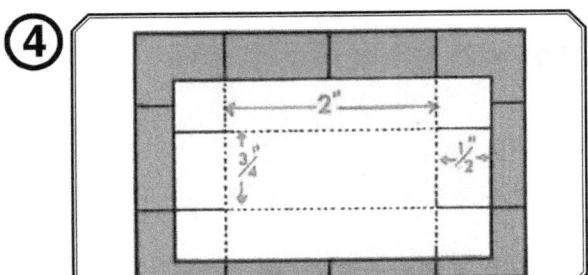

Draw and cut pattern for cistern from card 3" × 1¾". Fold on dotted lines and glue together. Paint on handle.

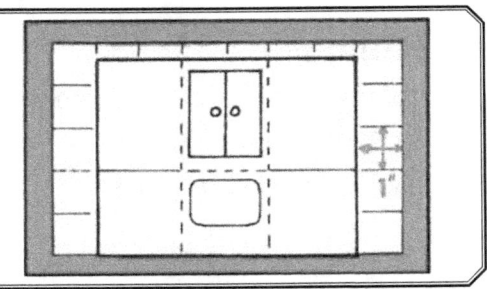

Draw and cut pattern for cupboard from card 6" × 4½". Fold along dotted lines and glue. Decorate as shown.

44

Colour Spin and Carousel

Materials Required

Colour Spin
* Disc of stiff card 3" diameter
* 2 ft. of thin string
* Scissors, coloured paints

Carousel
* Disc of stiff paper 16" diameter
* Two discs of stiff card 6" diameter
* Pencil, sharpened at both ends
* Corks
* Strip of stiff paper
* Sheets of coloured paper
* Glue and Cellotape
* Scissors, Coloured paints

Colour Spin

①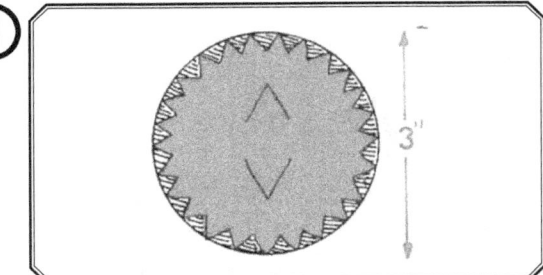

Cut triangular pieces from the outside of the disc, as shown.

②

Make 2 small holes, ½" on each side of the centre of the disc. Cut V shaped notches where indicated.

③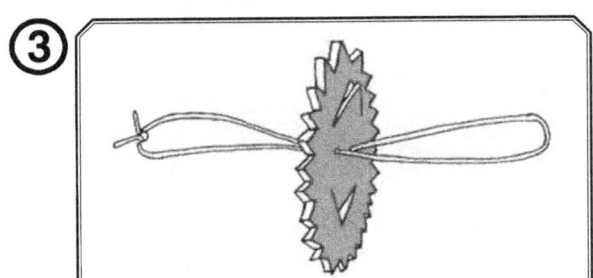

Thread string through. Make 2 loops as shown, and tie ends together.

④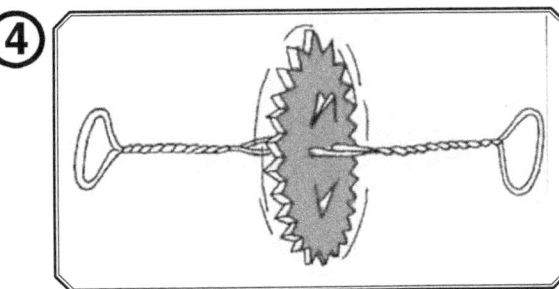

Hold a loop in each hand. Twist the disc to wind the string. Then pull the string and make it spin.

Carousel

①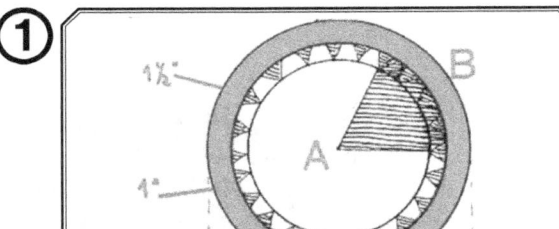

Cut out the red and shaded areas shown on the 16" disc of paper. Save outer piece (B) for later.

②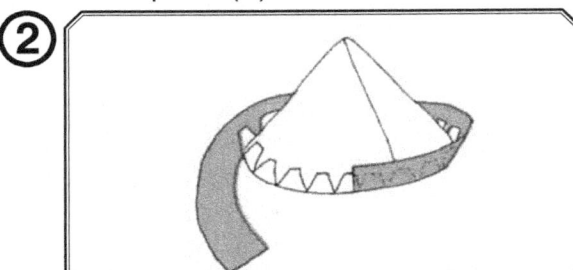

Fold and glue (A) into a cone. Fold tabs upwards, and glue strip of paper (B) around outside.

③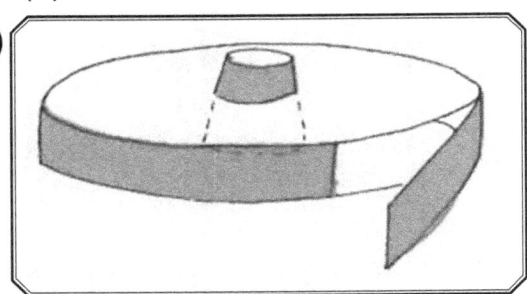

Cut a hole in the 6" disc to fit the cork. Glue other disc to base. Glue other disc to base. Glue paper strip around base.

④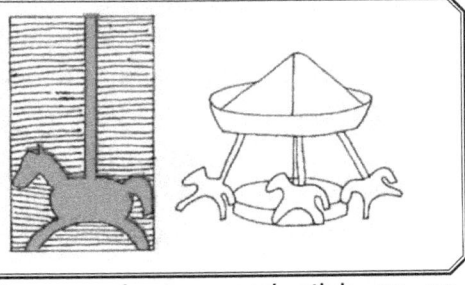

Cut paper horses and stick on as shown. Push one end of pencil in cork, balance roundabout on other.

45

Sunflower and Dahlia

Materials Required

Sunflower

- Cardboard disc 6" diameter
- Three 14" squares of yellow paper
- 2 ft. of ¼" dowel or tree twig
- Ball of dark brown wool
- Glue
- Cellotape
- Scissors

Dahlia

- Three discs of coloured paper 5" diameter
- 9" piece of wire
- Green paper for leaves
- Glue
- Pencil, scissors, Cellotape

Sunflower

①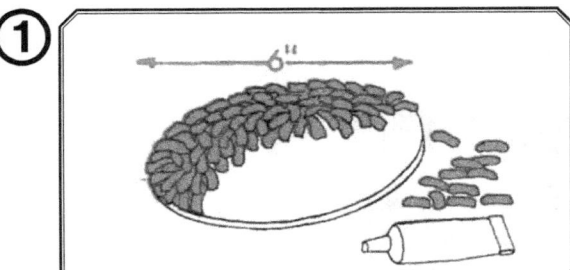
Cut wool into short lengths, approx. ½". Glue piece to one side of 6" disc.

②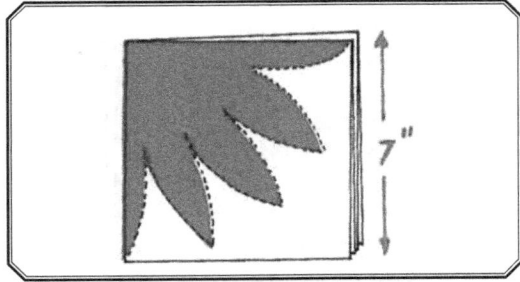
Fold yellow tissue paper into 7" squares. Cut pattern from open sides for petals and open out.

③
Glue the three pieces of yellow tissue paper to back of disc and arrange as shown.

④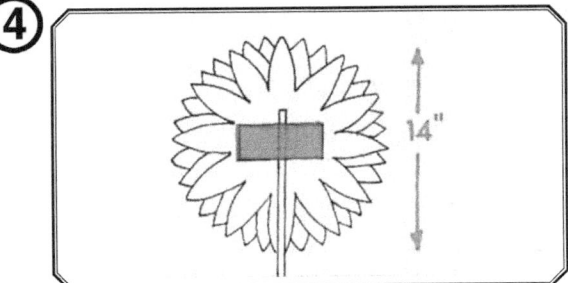
Tape stick or branch to back of flower.

Dahlia

①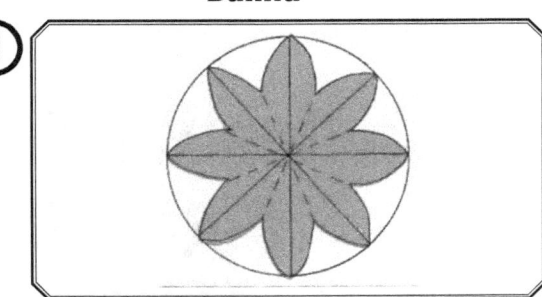
Draw and cut pattern for flower. Fold along solid lines.

②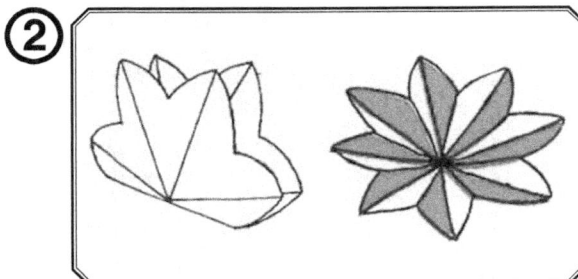
Open out, turn over and fold along dotted lines as shown.

③
Make 2 more. Thread wire through centres and bend down to secure. Arrange petals to make completed flower.

④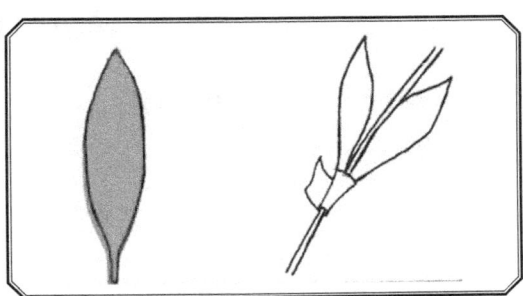
Draw and cut pattern for leaves and tape to stem.

46

Cotton Wool Snowman and Cotton Wool Chick

Materials Required

Cotton Wool Snowman
* Piece of thin coloured card 5" × 9"
* Piece of black paper 3" square
* White cotton wool
* Glue, pencil
* Scissors

Cotton Wool Chick
* Piece of coloured card 5" × 6"
* Piece of orange card 2" square
* Yellow cotton wool
* Glue, pencil
* Scissors

Cotton Wool Snowman

①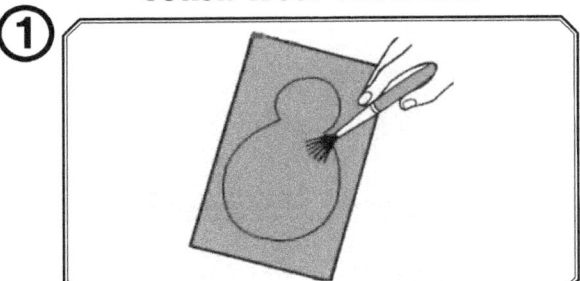
Draw shape of snowman on 5" X 9" card and glue this area.

②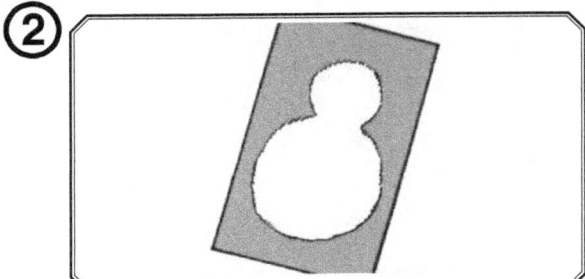
Press on small piece of cotton wool for head and large piece for body.

③
Draw and cut out shapes for hat, pipe, buttons and eyes from black paper.

④
Glue shapes in position to complete snowman.

Cotton Wool Chick

①
Draw shape of chick on 5" X 6" paper and glue this area.

②
Press on small piece of cotton wool for head and large piece for body.

③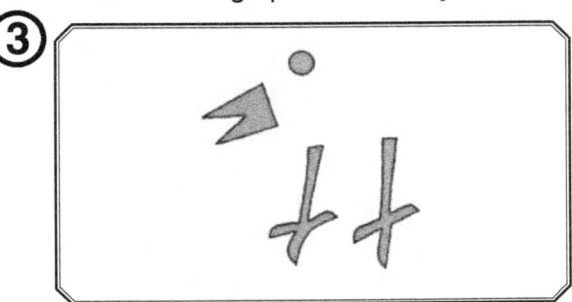
Draw and cut out shapes for legs, eyes and beak from orange card.

④
Glue shapes in position to complete chick.

47

Decorating the Rooms (Part 10)

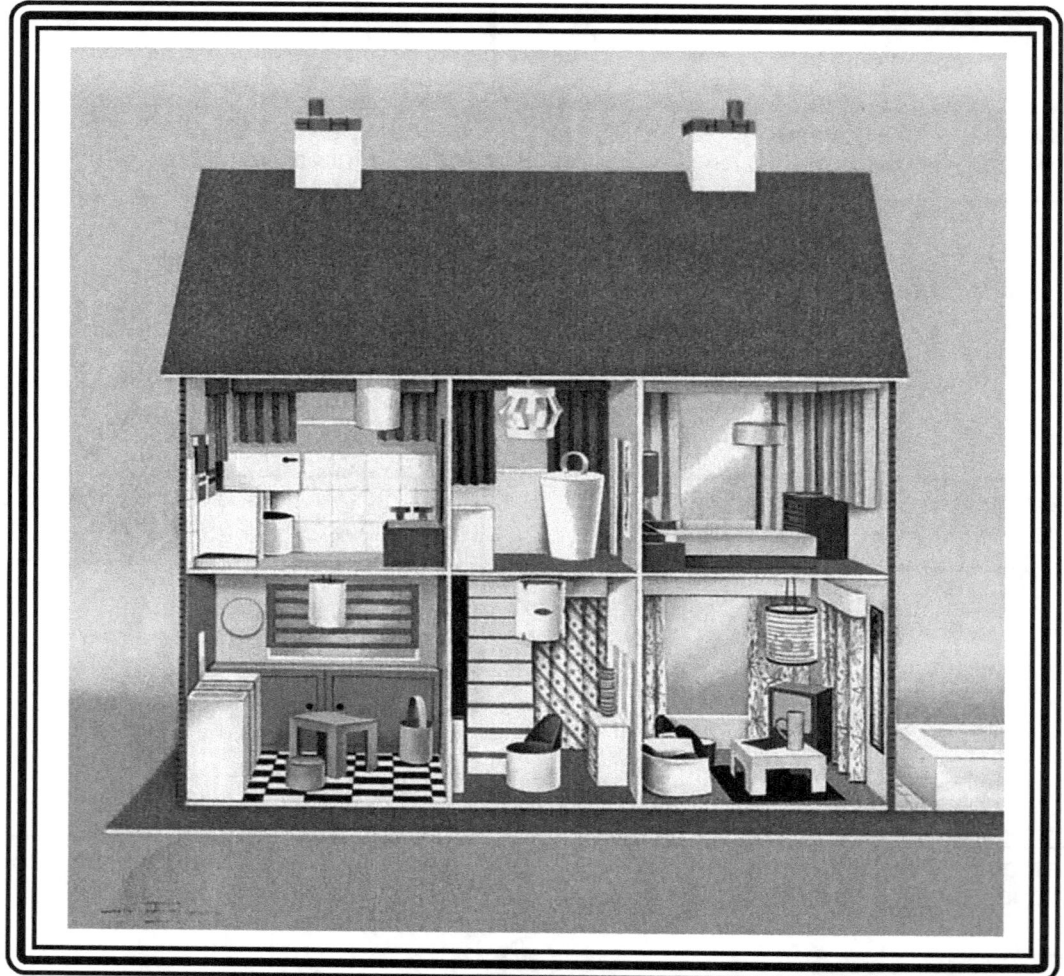

Materials Required

* Thin card
* Scissors, glue
* Needle and thread
* Cellotape
* Coloured paper

①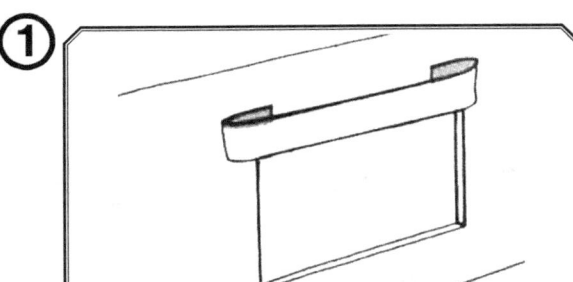

For pelmets cut a strip of paper ½" longer than the window. Bend at ends and glue as shown.

②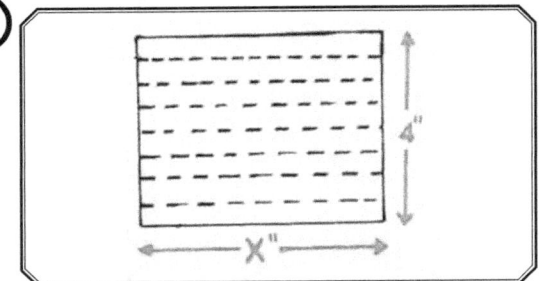

To make curtains fold pieces of coloured paper X" × 4", as shown (X is the depth of the window plus 1")

③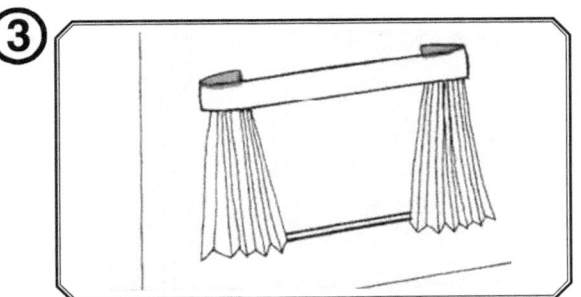

Gather curtains together at the top and tape. Glue inside pelmet as shown.

④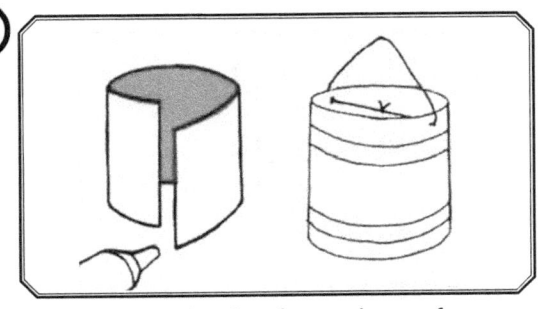

Make lampshades from piece of paper 1¼" × 3½" as shown. Loop on threads and tape them to the ceilings.

⑤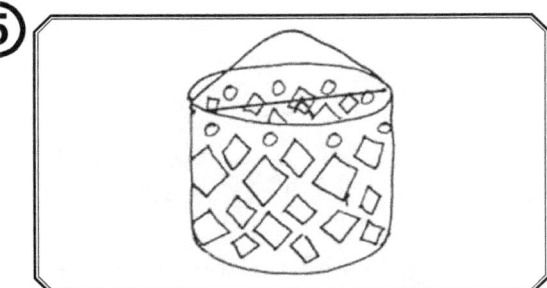

To make lampshades more attractive, cut some small holes in them before gluing together.

⑥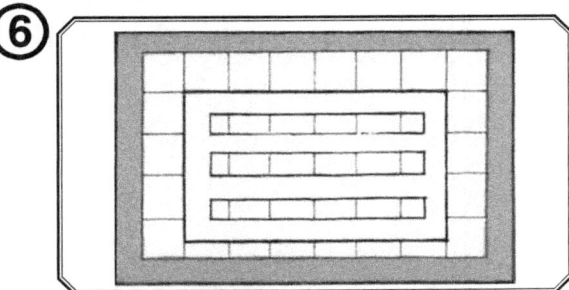

For Venetian blinds, draw and cut pattern from coloured paper. Glue them on inside of windows.

⑦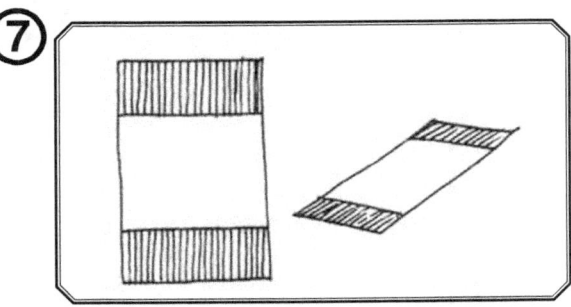

For rugs use piece of coloured paper 3" ×2" and cut a fringe at each end.

⑧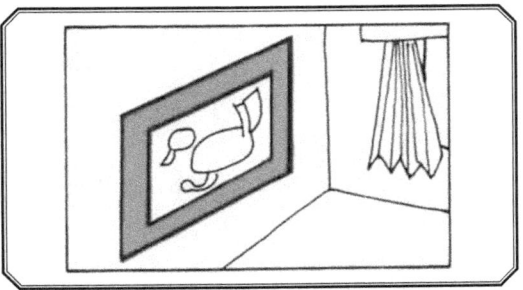

Cut small pictures from magazines, glue them on larger pieces of coloured paper to make frames, and glue to wall.

48
Magic Tree and Elephant Wall Frieze

Materials Required

Magic Tree
* Large piece of green paper
* (Newspaper will do)
* Scotch tape
* Scissors

Elephant Wall Frieze
* Three strips of coloured paper 12" × 3"
* Drawing pins
* Ruler
* Pencil
* Scissors, Coloured paints

Magic Tree

①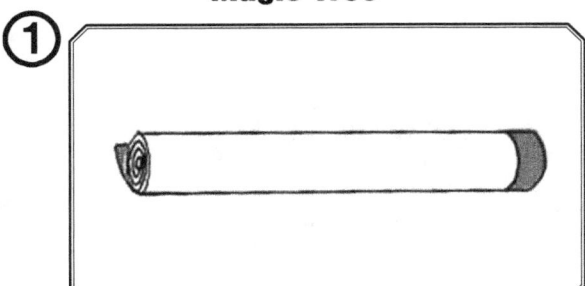
Roll paper into a tight tube and tape end as shown.

②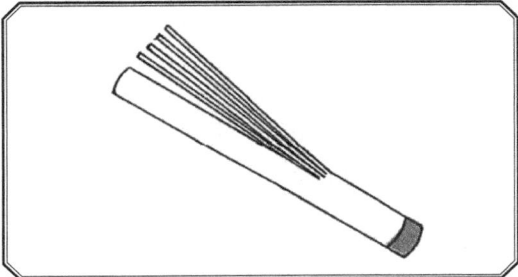
Cut down the tube to make strips, to within about 4" from the taped end.

③
Keep doing this until you have cut strips all around the tube.

④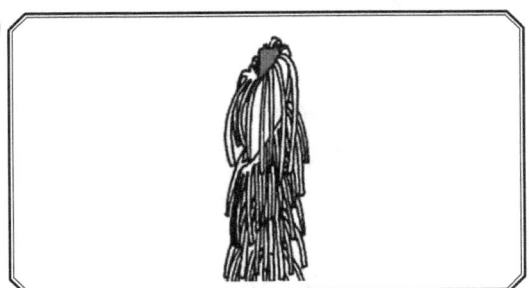
Bend strips down and pull upwards from centre. Watch your tree grow.

Elephant Wall Frieze

①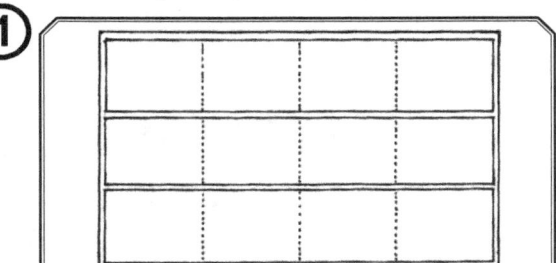
Mark the pattern above on your 12" X 3" paper strip and fold along the dotted lines.

②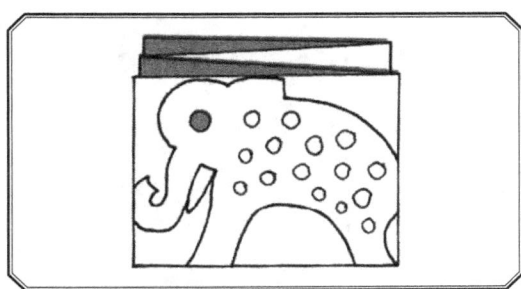
Fold each piece of paper into 4 as shown, and draw elephants on the top of each folded piece.

③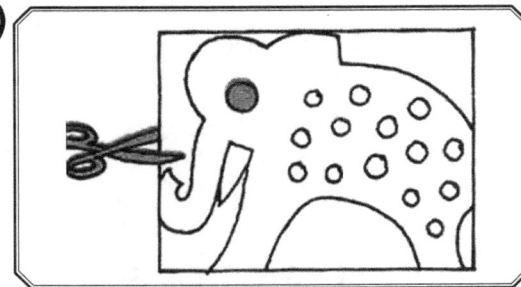
Cut out the patterns. Make sure that there is an uncut piece at each side.

④
Paint the elephants and tape the three strips together. Pin the coloured friezes along the top of your wall.

49

Lantern and Paper Necklace

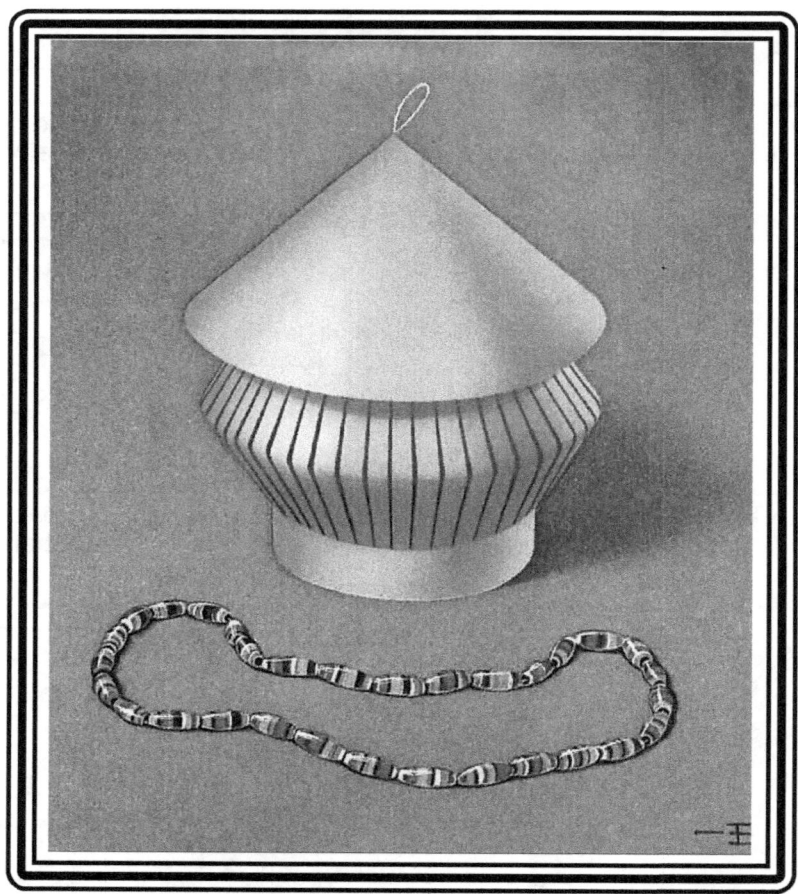

Materials Required

Lantern
* Coloured paper 18" × 8"
* Disc of coloured paper 12" diameter
* Wool
* Glue
* Pencil, ruler, scissors

Paper Necklace
* An old coloured magazine
* Glue
* Thread
* Scissors or good penknife
* Knitting needle

Lantern

①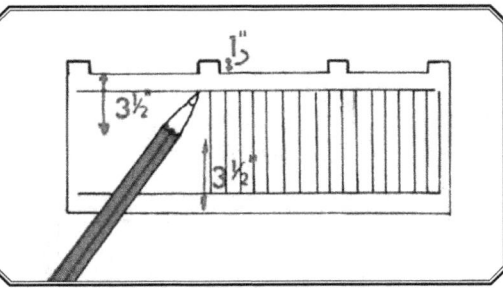
Draw pattern above on paper. Draw vertical lines ½" apart, as shown.

②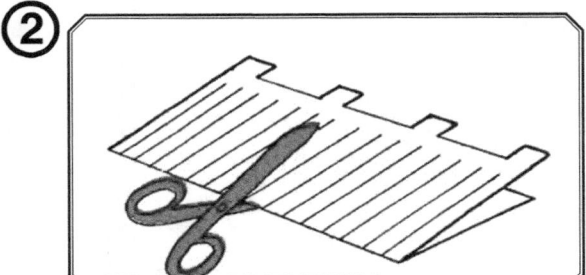
Fold along the dotted line and cut as shown.

③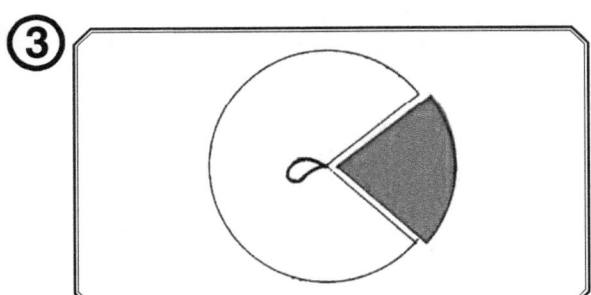
Cut to centre of 12" paper circle. Cut out segment, add knotted loop of wool, then glue to make cone.

④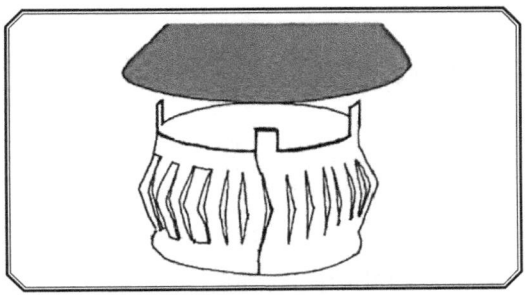
Open the paper strip and glue ends together. Then tape tabs inside top. Hang lantern up.

Paper Necklace

①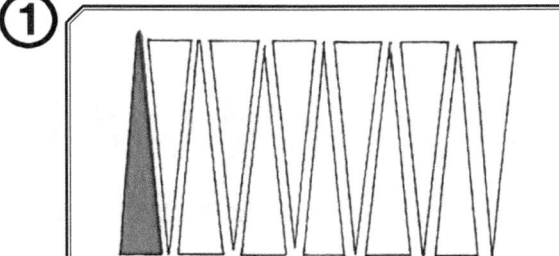
Mark and cut 18 triangular shapes from a coloured magazine picture 1" at the base and 10" long.

②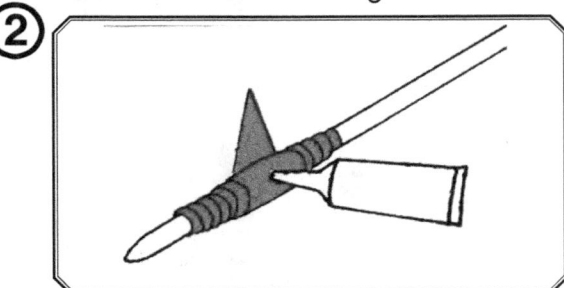
Put the large end of the triangle around a knitting needle. Roll it up and glue the point.

③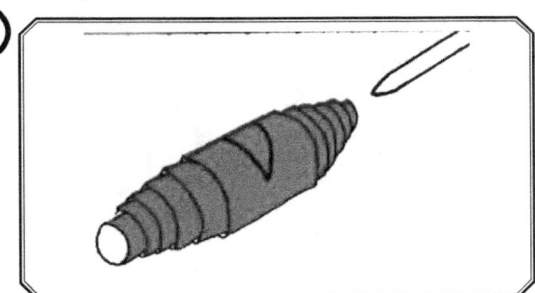
Hold until glue sets then pull needle out. This is one bead. Now make another 17 beads.

④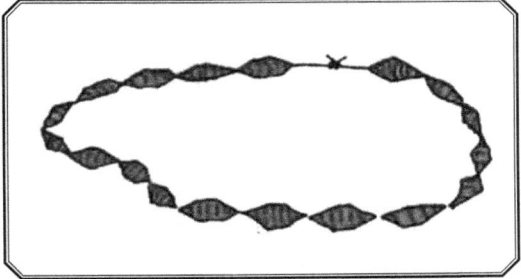
When all your beads are made, push the thread through them and tie the ends together.

50
Apple Cat and Potato Hedgehog

Materials Required

Apple Cat
* One large apple
* One small apple
* Two flat lolly sticks
* Two drawing pins
* Eight used matches

Potato Hedgehog
* One large potato
* One small potato
* Two thumbtacks
* Enough used matches to cover both potatoes

Apple Cat

①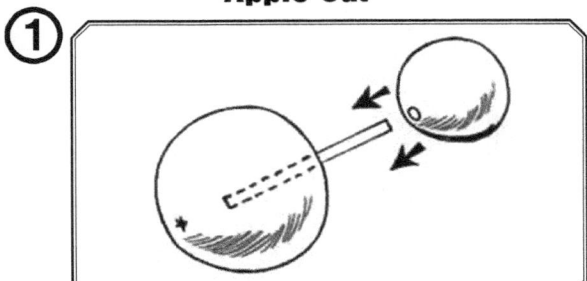
Push match halfway into large apple as shown. Than make small hole in small apple and fit onto match.

②
Cut lolly sticks in half and push into apples to make front paws and ears.

③
Add drawing pins for eyes.

④
Add remaining match-sticks for whiskers and tail.

Potato Hedgehog

①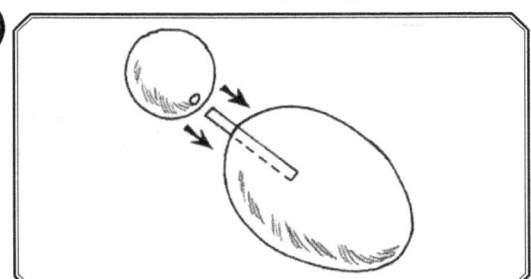
Push a match into large potato. Make small hole in small potato and fit onto match as shown.

②
Add drawing pins for eyes and four matches for legs.

③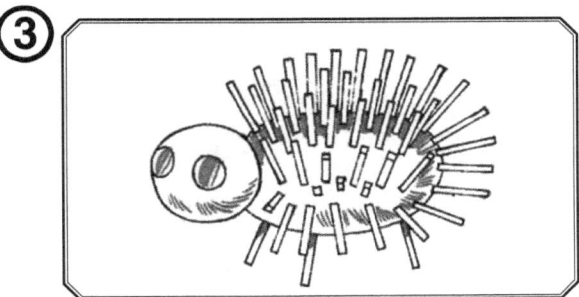
Push matches into body for spines.

④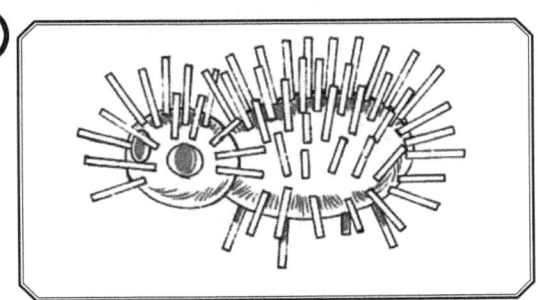
Push matches into head to complete.

51
Egg Box Models

Materials Required

* Egg boxes
* Pipe Cleaners
* Glue or Cellotape
* Good penknife, scissors
* Coloured paints

①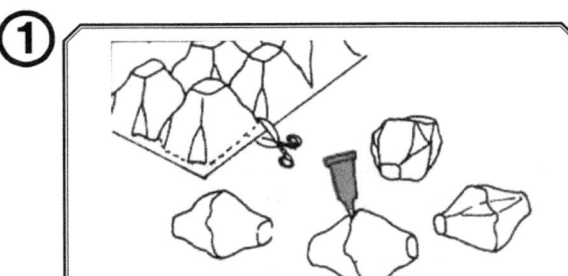
Cut eight segments from egg boxes and glue them together in pairs.

⑤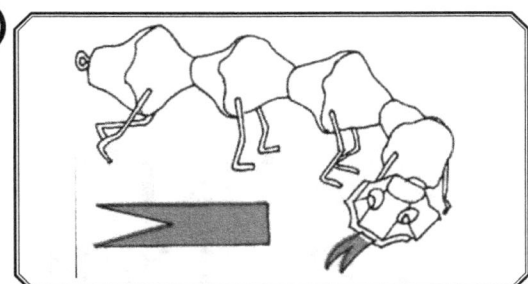
Cut pattern for tongue from box and glue to mouth. Paint and decorate your egg box dragon.

②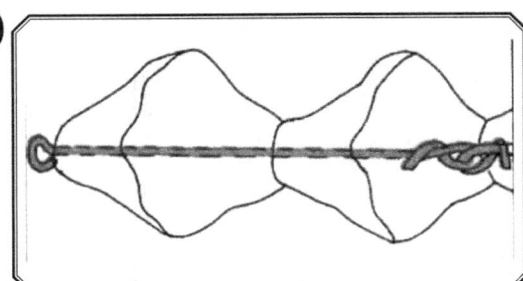
Pierce holes in ends and thread four sections together with pipe cleaners.

⑥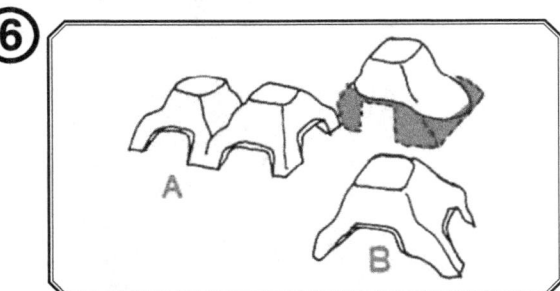
To make a camel (A) and an octopus (B), cut your egg box as shown.

③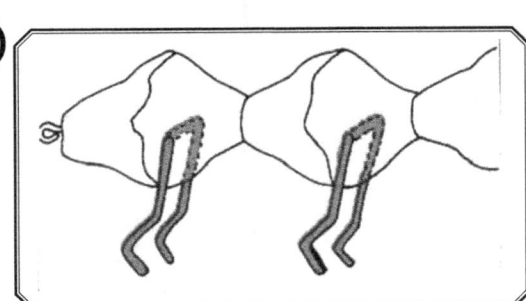
Pierce holes in sides of each section. Insert pipe cleaners and bend to make legs.

⑦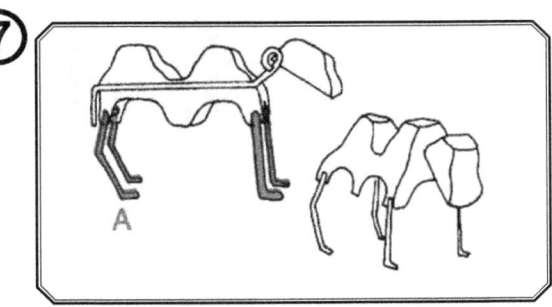
Join head to body of camel with a pipe cleaner. Make holes at sides and insert pipe cleaners for legs.

④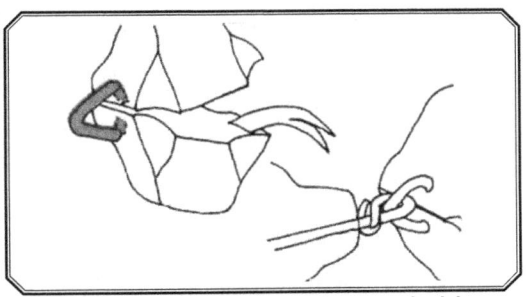
Cut 2 more segments and hinge together with pipe cleaner for head. Join to body as shown.

⑧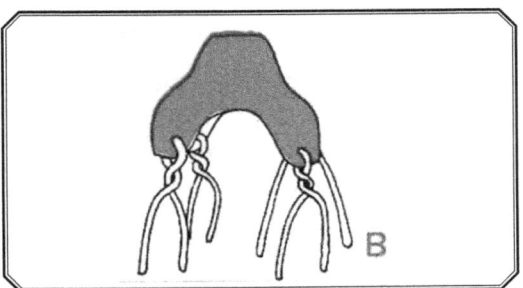
For octopus make holes in bottom corners. Insert cleaners and twist to make tentacles. Decorate camel and octopus with paints.

52

Pressed Flower Pictures and Pressed Flower Greeting Card

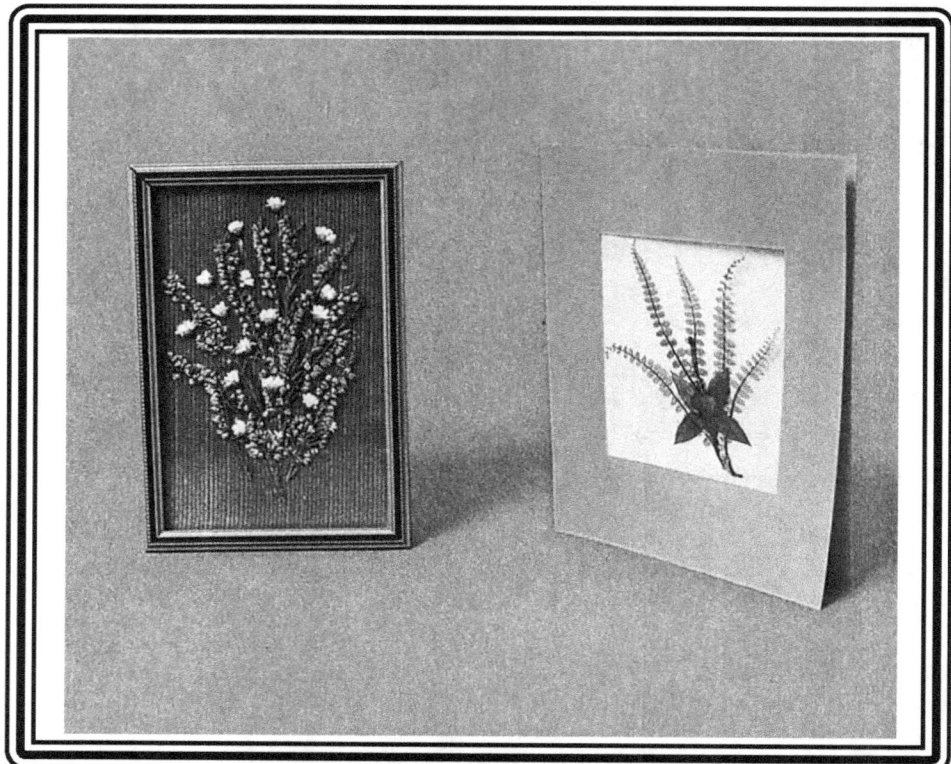

Materials Required

Pressed Flower Picture

* Piece of card size as requried
* Flowers and leaves
* Old newspapers
* Heavy books
* Glue

Pressed Flower Greeting Card

* Piece of coloured paper 11" × 13"
* Piece of "Cellophone" paper 4" × 5"
* Flowers and leaves
* Old newspapers
* Heavy book
* Glue, scissors
* Ruler, coloured pencil

Pressed Flower Picture

①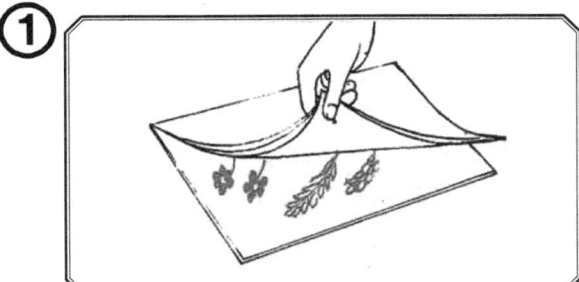
Carefully place flowers and leaves between several sheets of newspaper.

②
Put the newspaper in the middle of a heavy book. Place more books on top of this as extra weight and leave for 3 weeks.

③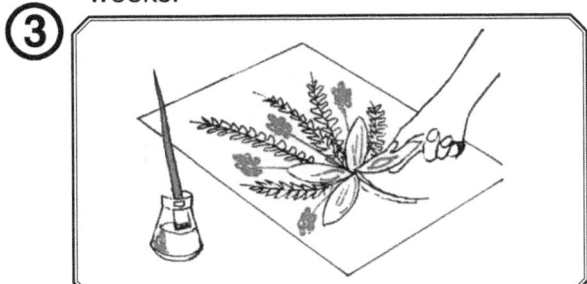
Carefully take out the pressed flowers and glue them onto the card.

④
Try to make them look as if they are growing. Put picture in frame or punch holes in top and hang with string.

Pressed Flower Greeting Card

①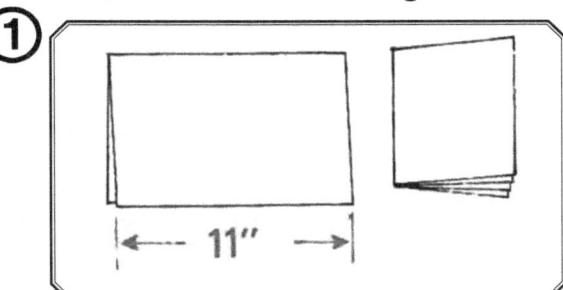
Fold coloured paper in half and then fold in half again. Open out flat then cut a 3" X 4" panel out of the top right segment.

②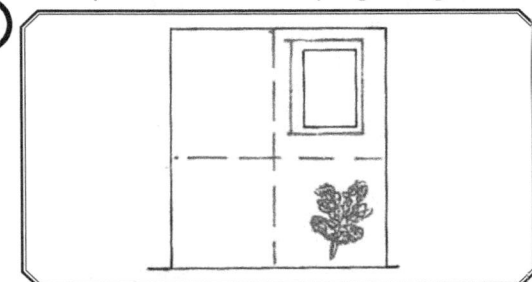
Glue "Cellophane" over hole. Draw 3" X 4" panel in bottom right segment. Arrange and glue pressed flowers and leaves onto the panel.

③
Fold paper so that flowers can be seen through "Cellophane" window.

④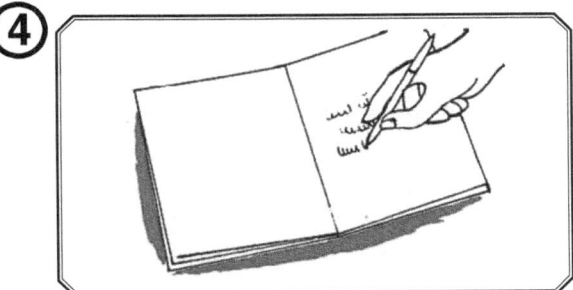
Write a message in the middle of your card.

53

Kaleidoscope

Materials Required

- Stiff card 12" long × 6½" wide
- Tin foil 12" long × 6" wide
- Piece of card 3½" square
- Piece of card 3" square
- Two pieces of "Cellophane" 3" square
- Glue and Cellotape
- White paint
- Transparent coloured beads
- Pencil, scissors, good penknife

①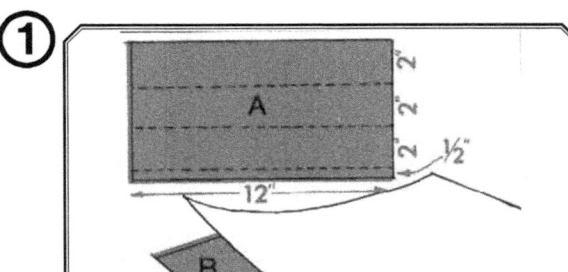
Draw dotted lines on one side of 12" X 6½" card in positions shown, and glue tin foil on other side.

②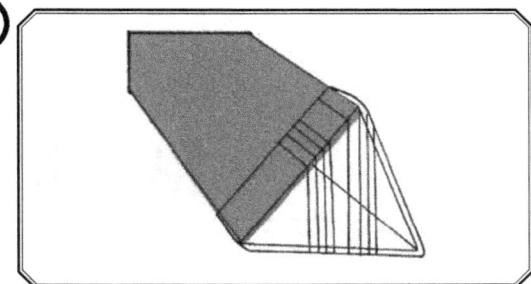
Bend along lines so that foil is inside. Glue flap outside.

③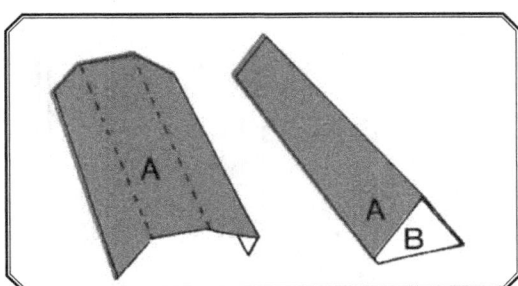
Draw and cut out pattern from 3" square of card. Make small peephole in centre.

④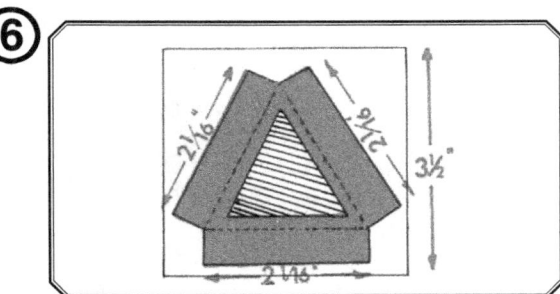
Glue tabs inside one end of triangular tube.

⑤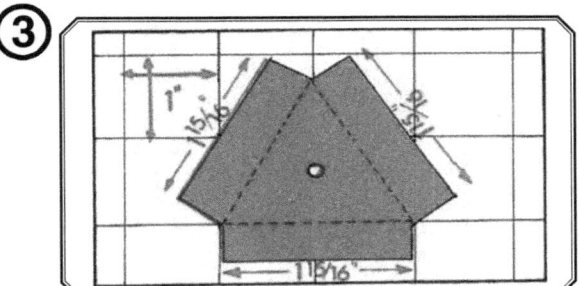
Carefully glue a piece of clear "Cellophane" over the other end of the tube.

⑥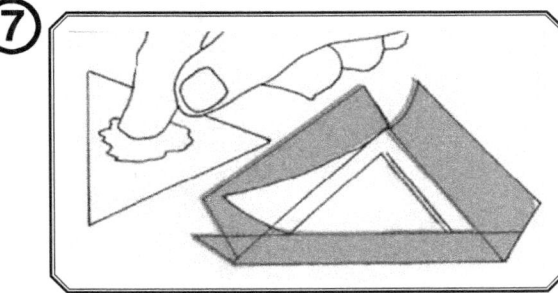
Draw and cut pattern from 3½" square of card. Cut triangular 'window' with good penknife.

⑦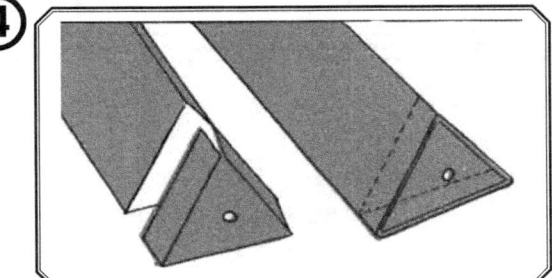
Carefully glue a triangle of "Cellophane" over window. Rub a dab of white paint on outside when glue is dry.

⑧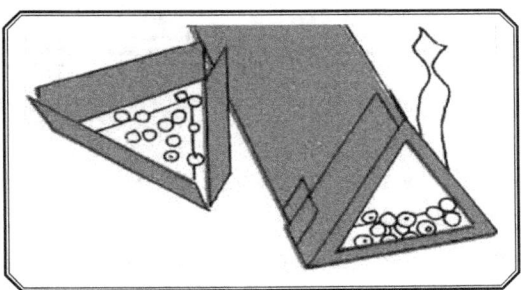
Put coloured beads in this cup and tape it to end of tube. Shake gently. Look through peephole.

54

Jacob's Ladder

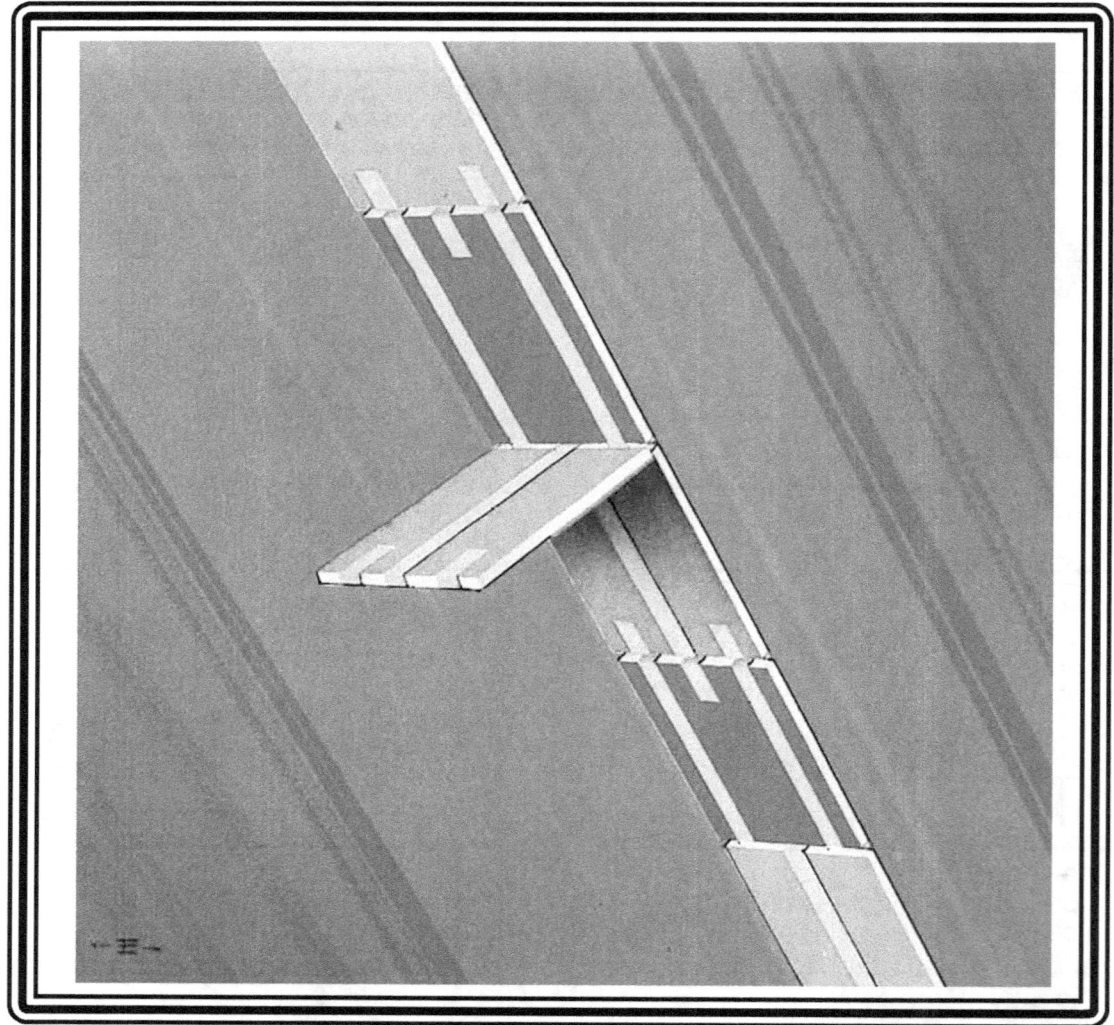

Materials Required

- Twelve pieces of very thick card 3" × 2"
- Five yards of ½" wide cloth tape
- Glue
- Scissors
- Coloured paints

①
Paint one side of each card blue and the other red. Cut tape into 40 pieces 4 1½" long

⑤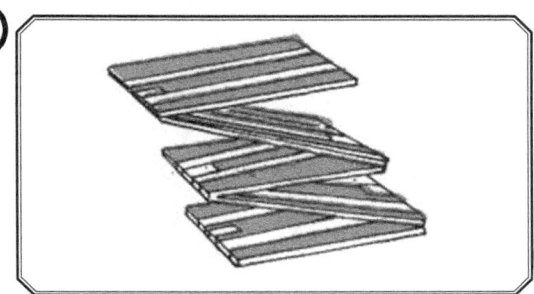
Join all the cards in this way, leaving the card with no tapes until last. Leave glue to set.

②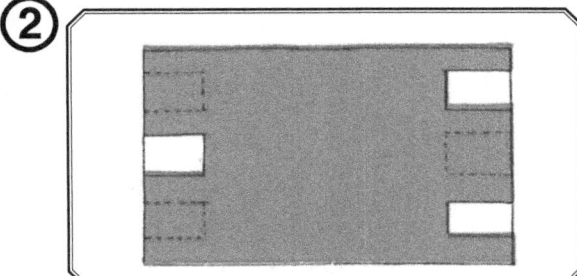
Mark cards on red sides as shown. Mark on blue sides at opposite edges. (See dotted lines.)

⑥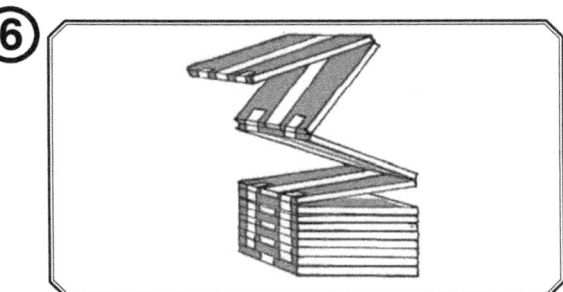
Fold the ladder. Then take the two top steps and open the ladder.

③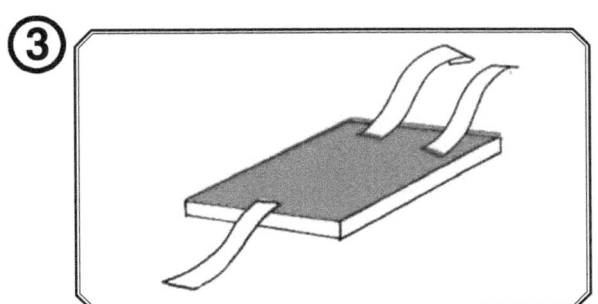
Glue three strips of tape onto every red side but one.

⑦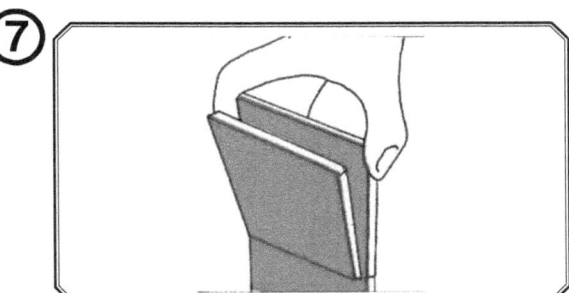
Open two steps and hold with finger and thumb as shown.

④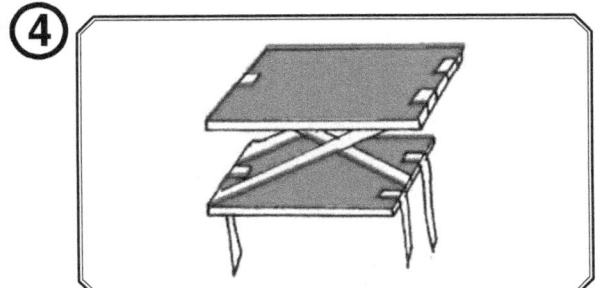
Take tapes under each card and glue to the marks on blue side of the next card.

⑧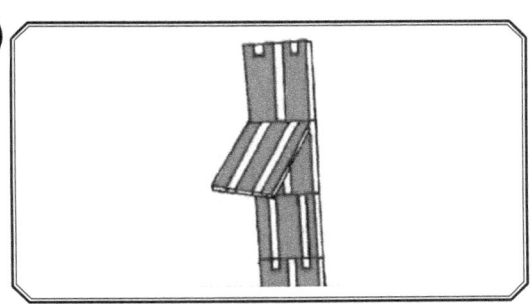
Let the second step fall, and see what happens!

www.ingramcontent.com/pod-product-compliance
Lightning Source LLC
Chambersburg PA
CBHW080553230426
43663CB00015B/2821